2007.

Dear Andrew;

This book is written by Tracy's twin sister, Linda. Their family was involved in starting TONKA toys in the U.S.

I hope you enjoy!

Best wishes for 2008,

Maureen

CIVIL WAR IN THE AMERICAN WORKPLACE

By Dr. Linda R. Rosene

Authors Choice Press
San Jose New York Lincoln Shanghai

Civil War in the American Workplace
How to Reduce Conflict at Work

Authors Choice Press
an imprint of iUniverse.com, Inc.

For information address:
iUniverse.com, Inc.
5220 S 16th, Ste. 200
Lincoln, NE 68512
www.iuniverse.com

Originally published by Self-published

Credit for Graphic: Dr. Linda R. Rosene

Although the author and publisher have made every
effort to ensure the accuracy and completeness of information contained in this book, any slights of people,
places, or organizations are unintentional.

ISBN: 0-595-18690-4

Printed in the United States of America

DEDICATION

This book is dedicated to Ralph, my husband, who encouraged me to enter the world of business and industry.

ACKNOWLEDGMENTS

There are many people to thank who contributed to my original concept of bringing psychological-mindedness to the North American workplace. Our many business clients added immeasurably to the richness of this book by their courage and willingness to share with us their organizational lives. Though their names are held in confidence, they may recognize their stories in the book as they read through its chapters. I thank them all. Without them, this book could have never been written.

My special thanks go to Lynn E. Baker and Bill Roberts, my family, who gave me the gift of seeing our family business, Tonka Toys, become world famous for quality toys. Dr. Jerry Nims, Virginia Satir, Meryl Tullis, Ron Hinrich, and Kathleen Peil were my first mentors in the world of clinical psychology. Their unrelenting generosity and early belief in my talents offered me rich educational and life experiences. I am especially indebted to Dr. Donald J. MacIntyre, Ph.D., President of Fielding Institute, who took valuable time to read the manuscript. He offered excellent suggestions that added clarity to the final version of the book.

I commend Bruce Hubby, President of the Professional Dynametric Program; Dr. Gerald L. Borofsky of Bay State Psychological Associates;

and Charlie Wonderlic, Jr., of Wonderlic Personnel Test, Inc. for their contributions to the development of state-of-the-art psychometric business testing instruments widely used throughout the world.

Bob Hitching, consultant to Target Systems, galvanized my focus and energies to finally begin writing my first book.

The Target Systems staff offered me encouragement and their support. My thanks go to all of them who took their time away from the office to read the manuscript and offer their helpful suggestions. Special thanks go to Robin Cala, Pam Howard, and Sheran Dunigan for their editing and formatting excellence. Robin also lent his special talents as the book's artist. The helpfulness, thoroughness, and diligence of these three TSI staffers are indicative of the best of their Herostyles. I relied heavily on their advice, which was always on-target.

Lastly, I give thanks to my husband Ralph, for his patience with my single-mindedness in getting the book written.

PREFACE

Since the publication in 1996 of Civil War in the American Workplace, Dr. Rosene's company, Target Systems, Inc., was sold to U.S. Personnel, Inc., a Professional Employee Organization. U.S. Personnel, Inc. is the twelfth largest PEO in the nation.

Located in Dallas-Fort Worth, Texas, U.S. Personnel, Inc. is an employee-leasing organization, providing business clients a wide array of employee administration and business consultative services. Dr. Rosene and her husband, Ralph Rosene, have been retained by U.S. Personnel, Inc. as Executive Consultants, to work with select organizations.

As they consult throughout North America, the Rosenes continue to find that the difference between "just average" organizations and successful organizations are those companies who successfully recruit, train, and retain talented, productive employees.

Unfortunately, too many organizations pour millions of dollars into employee recruitment, only to experience unacceptable levels of employee turnover. Keeping productive, talented employees requires leaders who take the time to understand the principles of human behavior as well as the motivational needs of their employees.

The messages found in Civil War in the American Workplace are highly relevant for today's readers.

In today's work world, employees are more interested in building their own successful careers rather than just working to make corporations profitable. Company leaders must be skilled at building employee trust in order to retain talented workers who are focused on the future successes of their organizations.

Civil War in the American Workplace can also help employees learn what makes their bosses "tick." This book is packed with helpful relationship-building information for leaders, employees, and work teams alike.

Civil War in the American Workplace is a reader-interactive book. In Chapter Two, readers are invited to complete an adjective checklist developed by Dr. Rosene. Following instructions, readers will discover which model of behavior fits them. Using real life business stories, Dr. Rosene's book humorously illustrates the psychological principles that guide human behavior.

Readers applying the behavioral principles found in Civil War in the American Workplace can find themselves working more effectively with and for others. This book is an answer for those who want to enjoy their world at work.

TABLE OF CONTENTS

CIVIL WAR
IN THE
AMERICAN
WORKPLACE

By Dr. Linda R. Rosene

INTRODUCTION

I entered the world of corporations after leaving my clinical practice in 1983. Before that time, I had consulted with clinical clients in mental health agencies covering family issues as well as business issues. When couples had difficulties in their marriages or family relationships, the problem often spilled over into their work or businesses.

Having lived with a corporate executive for more than 20 years gave me practical insight into the world of work that my clinical clients found helpful. The more work I did with client businesses, the more I realized my impact was greater in bringing solutions to many rather than to few. As the boss got better in his or her ability to communicate with the family, so too did the ability to manage employees. As the boss's skills for management increased, so did the employees' sense of being valued. It was with great satisfaction that I saw people "get better" as a result of my interventions.

When my husband, Ralph, and his partner offered me the opportunity to become a full-time consultant in their organization, Target Systems, Inc. (TSI), it seemed a natural extension to what I had enjoyed most in my private practice. I jumped at the opportunity.

So, in 1983, I began to develop Target Systems' Human Resource Department and add to Ralph and his partner's strategic planning and operations skills the ingredient of psychological understanding of people in the workplace. It has proven to be the most important move of my professional career. However, little did I realize the battlefield I was entering!

The corporate field has had its share of charlatans. I have shared many a dais with people with little skill for helping employers wage the battle of global competitiveness. They offered immediate relief, the quick cure, the easy out, the one-time fix-it technique, or human resource product. What they were in the business of, was staying in business! Many of these individuals had worked for others, but were now self-employed. Unfortunately, from their experiences, they only had a short view of the challenges facing American corporations. What they did not seem to understand was the complexity of the problems facing their listeners. Nor did they appear to understand the psychological complexities of their audiences.

What I had gained as a psychologist in living and working with my husband, Ralph—a strategic organizational developer and planner—was the long view of corporate survival. From him I learned there is no easy answer facing corporate executives. The saddest part of my work, however, has been watching executive after executive search for the instant fix. They want to feel better, today! Their fear of change, of doing business differently, of giving up established work relationships, or of dealing with their company's "sacred cows" is too much. Their anxiety levels push for relief! I know, however, if the answer is easy, it is probably wrong.

Besides surviving the economic struggle into the twenty-first century, leadership survival requires leaders to listen to their employees, read between the lines, and think critically for themselves about how to meet the challenges facing their organizations.

Years ago in a national business journal, we were called "the company that would lead the retail industry kicking and screaming into the twenty-first century." That job has not always been a popular one. No one wants to hear that they must hold every employee accountable to bottom-line results or they may not survive as a company. Additionally, many corporate executives lack "natural skills" for leading their organizations through the battlefields of corporate civil war. Levinson (1994) finds too many executives in Fortune 500 companies ill-suited for the challenges facing their organizations. Family-run businesses are no different. Not only are family members often ill-suited to naturally run their companies, but too many family-run businesses in the country today make decisions on what is best for their families, rather than what is best for their companies.

Corporate survival requires courage of all of us. Courage to become what our companies need for us to be; to learn new skills; to interact with others in different, more tolerant ways; to make tough decisions required of leaders; and to always assess our corporate decisions based on what is best for our customers. For executives buried deep in their family's history, this may prove too harrowing a challenge.

Founders of Tonka Toys

As a child, I witnessed the making of a king, a corporate king to be specific. In 1948, my uncle, Lynn Baker, through good luck, brilliant analysis, and sacrifice, began a small toy company in an old school house. His good luck was his timing. World War II had ended triumphantly for the Western World and men returned in droves eager for normalcy and the love of their families. Uncle Lynn's brilliance was taking advantage of a world at peace, the abundance of wartime steel, and cheap labor— all of which had become available to those enterprising enough to find a peaceful use for this available resource.

Seeing an abundance of cheap steel and an abundance of women who had learned the rewards of working outside their homes and were still eager to be employed, my Uncle Lynn gambled his entire life savings. He began a steel toy manufacturing company on the shores of Minnesota's Lake Minnetonka.

Uncle Lynn, without benefit of expensive demographers or marketers, instinctively knew he had a possible shot at cashing in on the desires of millions of men and women who, tired of war, were now eager to enjoy the fruits of their war sacrifices. They made babies, millions of them.

Between 1946 and 1965, 78 million babies were born, the largest population of new citizens in the history of the United States. Their population cohort became famous as the Baby Boomer generation.

The parents of Baby Boomers lavished attention *and toys* on their children! My uncle's toy manufacturing business burst onto this prolific, energetically generous scene, and Tonka Toys became a smashing success.

As a young girl watching my uncle's family transform from middle class to royalty, the silent power of wealth awed me as it stole into our living room. Hushed crowds of men huddled in small groups waiting their audience with Uncle Lynn. Aunt Florence graciously moved among them having a smile for all and a cup of coffee ready to pour from her sterling coffee server. Never before had I seen so many men on weekends, dressed in expensive suits and wearing beautiful jewelry sitting about my family's living room. 1 knew without words that my family was discovering a new world.

In 1953, my father joined Tonka Toys as the Chief Operating Officer in charge of purchasing and personnel. A friendly man, my father was as different from Uncle Lynn as was possible. Uncle Lynn was imposing both in stature and in business relationships. Quietly powerful, he was short on small talk. Instead, his interests appeared to revolve around results and money. I saw him smile seldom. When he did, it was when my Aunt Florence was with him. His remoteness to me was paradoxically a powerful magnet. I loved just watching from the corner of the room, the dynamics of king-making.

My father, however, was at home with everyday things: work, his newspaper, good music, sports on the radio, and a keen sense of humor. He was loved by many. As the years went by, he became the heart of Tonka Toys. His employees, mostly women married to blue-collar workers, loved him. He gave credit to many and ignored very few. He was host to all the company parties with touching stories about the women who made Tonka Toys.

Disorganized, when Dad would finally clean his desk an announcement would duly be made over the manufacturing plant intercom, "Bill Roberts' desk is clean," and the women cheered. When one of the employees had a family tragedy, Dad would often come home with tears in his eyes. As a Tonka Toys man, he touched many people in a kind, gentle way.

In contrast, Uncle Lynn was held in awe from a distance by those around him. He was not to be bothered, for his time was "important." Self-contained and in his later years in poor health, Uncle Lynn was loved from afar. I knew even as a young girl, this was his most painful family sacrifice. His daughter and son missed having a dad. Instead, they had a father making dreams come true for generations of other people's children.

I intuitively knew the differences between my father and Uncle Lynn were necessary for Tonka Toys to thrive. I knew then there could only be one person like Uncle Lynn but not enough individuals like my father for Tonka Toys to grow. Uncle Lynn loved risk-taking and "deal-making." My father loved people and daily operations. This organizational chart partnership paid off handsomely for everyone involved.

When I was 11 years old, Uncle Lynn took me into one of the warehouses holding hundreds of thousands of Tonka Toy trucks waiting to be shipped for the December holidays. With an expansive wave of his arm, he said in a booming voice, "Pick out one for yourself!"

I was dumbstruck. First, I was the only girl in a family of boys. Second, Uncle Lynn had never offered me that choice before. With what seemed hours of agonizing waffling, I chose the semi-trailer truck with the "Jolly Green Giant" painted on a white background. As I write, I can still feel the weight of the box as I carried it out to the car.

As a family member, I felt a deep sense of pride as Tonka Toys became an international phenomenon. I had witnessed a transformation so profound as to be a twentieth century miracle. Hard work, hunches, good luck, and risk-taking did make a difference. I did not forget this lesson.

Even today, 40 years later, as I speak to audiences throughout North America, adult Baby Boomers and young Baby Busters proudly hold their hands high when I ask: Who has a Tonka Toy in their garage, attic, or closet? My Uncle Lynn's early dream still creates happy memories for millions of today's families.

Succession to Outsiders

"They agreed the toy company's survival was more important than serving the wishes of the family."

However painful a realization, I believe what made Tonka Toys a household word was the fact Uncle Lynn and my father agreed no second generation family member would succeed either one of them. They agreed the toy company's survival was more important than serving the wishes of the family. That meant both my cousin and my older brother were excluded from consideration when my uncle and father retired.

I did not realize it at the time, but this was a painful decision for my oldest brother. He had prepared himself for Tonka Toys throughout his college years and wanted to be considered by Uncle

Lynn as a plant manager-trainee. But he was turned down.

Instead, nonfamily and proven outside performers were hired and promoted into positions as Tonka Toys' next generation of leaders. Time itself has proven the wisdom of those early, difficult choices. Tonka Toys became a Fortune 100 company.

A powerful succession model was enacted that continues to have profound effects on how I view organizations. Uncle Lynn made a business decision that he believed was for the good of the company. It did not please several next generation family members. However, the veracity of Uncle Lynn's decision shows in Tonka Toys' continuing enjoyment of an international reputation almost 50 years after the company was founded.

"All performance comes from belief."

Having witnessed my family's founding of an international company led me to realize "all performance comes from belief." Today that phrase is our consulting company's driving force statement. There is nothing so powerful as self-belief, having the confidence and courage to act on one's abilities. Belief is often the determining factor in a company's will to succeed. Target Systems has worked to put into action this premise in those companies we now consult with. Without a strong and positive self-belief bolstering today's leaders, their leadership challenges would be formidable.

"There is nothing so powerful as self-belief, having the confidence and courage to act on one's abilities. Belief is often the determining factor in a company's will to succeed."

"All of the ingredients in a [business] that count are changeable and correctable--individual self-worth, communication, system, and rules--at any point in time. In fact, I would go so far as to say that any piece of behavior at a moment in time is the outcome of the four-way interplay of the person's self-worth and body condition of that moment, his interaction with another, his system, and his place in time and space and situation. If I have to explain his behavior, I have to say something about all these facts, not just one, and then I must also look to see how each part influences the other." - Virginia Satir, PEOPLE-MAKING, preface.

My belief in myself led me to enter graduate school seeking a Ph.D. in psychology when I was 40 years old. I lived out my Uncle Lynn's message to his family: Be what your instincts, talents, good luck, and natural resources allow!

My phenomenal good luck as a psychotherapist was having the privilege of working with the world renowned family therapist, Virginia Satir. Her approach to family therapy was riveting to observe and live! Virginia's core therapeutic belief was that individuals do not have enough choices in their lives. It is because of this self-imposed limitation of choices that we often become poor parents, poor life-mates, and poor friends to ourselves.

As a change agent, no one was as magical as Virginia. At the time of her death, she had gained an international reputation for successfully working with more than 45,000 families and groups effecting meaningful changes in their lives. People lived better because of their time spent with Virginia Satir.

Virginia's model for change incorporated psychological tenets of denial, repression, addiction, poor self-esteem, neurosis, and psychosis. However, Virginia presented these concepts to families and groups in nonthreatening language that allowed people to accept their need to change.

Early on, I became a willing student of Virginia's principles and working models. Her unfailing belief in people's resiliency and her unrelenting ability to smile, even when facing a raging family empowering them to change for the better, gave me the inspiration to become a psychologist.

Virginia's model of working with people and groups continues to guide my work. I have found even the most recalcitrant CEOs respond to positive psychological approaches which enables them to face the challenges of change.

"Most recalcitrant CEOs respond to positive psychological approaches which enables them to face the challenges of change."

As a result of my early childhood Tonka Toys experiences, my corporate experience with my husband, Ralph, and my family therapy experiences with Virginia Satir, I have gained an entrepreneurial, positive outlook and a "briefcase" of practical psychological skills that have led to my growing business reputation. I have enjoyed helping people move through their seemingly insurmountable business and family problems to successful resolutions.

I welcome you to expand your experience of personal choice and empowerment in finding more positive approaches for yourself in creating peace within your workplace civil wars.

How to Use This Book

This book is geared to reader interaction. Chapter Two contains a self-choice adjective checklist from which you, the reader, can select adjectives that most describe you. Once your adjective selection is complete, you will have a choice of four

13

behavioral models from which to choose. Choose the model that *best describes you*.

The remaining chapters of this book are descriptions of how individual behavior and perception influence beliefs and actions that occur in people during their time at work.

You can select adjectives that describe you in Chapter Two. Then *repeat* the exercise of adjective selection and match the adjectives with a person with whom you work. In this second exercise, you will understand yourself as well as those individuals that work alongside you or for you. By understanding behavior, yours and others, you will better address the civil war occurring in your workplace.

"Civilized" War

American business is in the midst of a civilized war. This war is not as easily defined as armed conflict as was the great bloodletting of the nineteenth century. But this workplace "civil" war perhaps equals past world wars for its potential for destruction. The workplace war surrounding us today is taking place in corporations and small businesses as people feel betrayed by each other and by the very system itself. This war is "civilized" in that no guns are fired and no enemy is executed. Included in this war are employees who are running scared and employers who are struggling to keep their organizations afloat by using modern restructuring theories.

As in all wars, brutal or "civilized," generals seek ways to create cease fires and make treaties. Judicial forums emerge to punish war criminals and set things straight for the next world order. In corporate civilized wars, the same process has emerged. We have the Total Quality Movement (TQM) experts skirmishing with their answers; the downsizers clearing out expendable workers; the reengineering people, the team conceptualizers, the flat organizational chart pushers, and the prophets of "empowerment" . . . yet the war continues.

In their rush to downsize in support of cost and bottom line, many executives have missed the need for product development, innovation, new markets, and growing rather than reducing their organizations.

Target Systems

CHAPTER ONE

CIVIL WAR IN THE AMERICAN WORKPLACE

Paradoxically, America is in a war to save something it has already lost. The battle is being waged in the world of work. More than ten million jobs have been permanently annihilated since 1989 and the bloodletting continues. Jobs, as the twentieth century worker knew it, are now becoming obsolete. Everyone fears the landscape of work. The corporate field is becoming a wasteland of broken dreams. We are in a war no one knows how to fight. The battle lines are fuzzy, the enemy may be us, but the outcome is certain. We will all work differently (and for less?) in the twenty-first century than did our twentieth century fathers and mothers. No longer will the American dream come true. The aspect of hard work in the next hundred years promises only sparing results and many risks. As in all wars, there will be a few generals at the top, served by their lieutenants. There will be the masses of foot soldiers struggling in the

Overlooked are the possibilities for people to add to the innovation and transformation of their organizations.

Target Systems

17

trenches against common enemies called: minimum wages, short work assignments, obsolete skills, reeducation, self-employment, and fear.

The generals are circling in their war rooms struggling to find how and where to secure a beachhead in the global economy.

Having realized that their charts, graphs, and tables are obsolete as predictors for investing and expansion, these warriors now seek new gurus and programs: TQM, Reengineering, Work Teams, and Employee Empowerment to give them time to reassess their damage control. Everyone feels the heat of the enemy, but no one has a clear war plan which can guarantee American corporations' continuation of "business as usual." Companies sell, buy, or merge, creating new groups of employees who are forced to establish unfamiliar beachheads and work relationships within the encampment, the new company entity.

Employers rue the lack of employee commitment in an era when they have zero or low commitment to their people.

Target Systems

We hunker down, hoping for the best, expecting the worst. We are circling our wagons, yet, our jobs as we know them, continue to disappear at an alarming rate.

As in all wars, today's "soldiers," the American workers, are becoming dehumanized as our generals wage economic battles required by global competition. Our corporate generals must deny us our humanhood for their own sanity. Otherwise, they would experience firsthand the tragedy they are visiting on the nation. Psychologically, individuals, whether they are leaders or follow-

18

ers, repress or deny reality to themselves when it becomes too painful. It is easier to turn to technology and technological processes as the new battle plans for winning the economic war rather than view the bloody carnage of unemployment. Increased use of computerization, robotics, and reengineering suggests the American worker has become expendable to the corporate generals. Why?

It is easier to shut down machines than merge new work groups or to permanently lay off millions of men and women. If this is so painful, why does this have to happen?

For over one hundred years, the American worker has enjoyed the American dream: work hard, earn more, and become wealthier than anyone living outside the United States could imagine. We believed in our abilities to secure "the good life" and became our own best customers of the goods we produced. When we could no longer consume what we created, we *exported* our excess wealth and grew even wealthier. No end was in sight. We euphorically sailed our seas not realizing that in these uncharted waters, there could be an edge over which the end would rise and suck us under. What happened?

The American worker has become too expensive to keep around. Hourly wages for American employees average well above those paid to Pacific Rim or Mexico workers. Natural resources are becoming limited and with the coming

"The 1980s can be viewed as the 'hardware' decade of rapid transformation, in which much of the organizational change in the United States was done via massive downsizing and restructuring..." - Haas, THE LEADER WITHIN.

Disillusion has set in. The American worker still wants meaningful work, yet meaning seems to elude their grasp. Since 1974 the average wage dropped from $8.55 to $7.54.

Target Systems

19

of virtual reality, time and space no longer pose a competitive barrier to a vibrant world economy.

Like everyone else, I experienced the shock of this shift in the American dream when I read that my children's generation, the Baby Boomers, would not enjoy the wealth of successes that their parents had. We, the "silent" generation, had the *good fortune* of having careers during the 1960s through the 1990s when America could pay us handsomely for our contributions. Now like everyone, I look ahead with a sense of "low grade anxiety," not knowing whether to be excited by the challenges or just to be scared silly!

We are like leaves on the wind, being blown by a force that is difficult to see. The best minds are studying the past and present to map the future. How accurate they prove to be, we cannot know today. Be assured you are not alone in your search for understanding today's economic and workplace struggles.

"Like everyone, I look ahead with a sense of 'low grade anxiety,' not knowing whether to be excited by the challenges or just to be scared silly!"

Useful Historical Models

I have dug deep into history to find answers in models that are not twentieth century American in origin, but concepts that have transcended history and culture. To do so, I have walked down

20

the corridors of history, through the winding roads of human behavior that go back to the roots of civilization as we now know it. In so doing, I went back to a place in Greek history where the very concepts of logic, reason, and being find their first tangible expression in written form. Aristotle gave us models that deal with cause and effect and have become the rational thought processes of today. Heraclitus gave us the truth that everything is changing except the truth that everything is changing. Others, such as Plato and Socrates, laid out ideas that still govern the way we perceive life.

Behavior's Role in the Workplace Civil War

It was in this era of thought that Hippocrates posited a definition that theorized all personalities could be categorized into four behavioral traits or temperaments. These four traits have an impact on the way we act, react, think, and feel. Understanding these four behavioral traits can help us to understand ourselves and others. Through increased levels of self-understanding of our behaviors, we can be proactive in improving all our interpersonal relationships, at work as well as at home. As we improve our interpersonal relationships at work, we can choose to reduce our work conflicts.

"Through increased self-understanding of our behaviors, we can be proactive in improving all our interpersonal relationships at work."

21

A basic tenet of this book is that by reducing our interpersonal work conflicts we can reduce our daily battles, our civil wars, being waged in American businesses. The purpose of this book is to give you information with which to gain increased self-knowledge and personal flexibility as an employee, manager, or owner, to experience greater choices by which to navigate your turbulent waters of economic, organizational, and global conflict.

"Hippocrates' four temperaments: sanguine (cheerful and active), melancholic (gloomy), choleric (angry and violent), and phlegmatic (calm and passive)." - Henry Gleitman, PSYCHOLOGY

To achieve this goal, use this book to "map" your behavioral style and those of people with whom you relate. The four behavioral traits first described by Hippocrates are very applicable to today's world. The concept of personality suggests our behavior is predictable and we can be counted on to act in certain ways given certain contexts. In the world of work, one's personality style or behavioral trait, then, becomes an elegant tool for understanding what causes us or others to act or not to act, to create conflict or resolve it.

The work structure is rapidly changing to one which requires intellectual skill. Jobs require a skilled, flexible, retrainable person who is able to embrace change and their responsibility to add value to the task and organization.

Target Systems

As the title of the book suggests, I am using military metaphors as a way to create understanding of the four behavioral styles presented in this book. Not that I am a militarist at heart, but all of us tend to understand military terminology because of our overexposure to twentieth century wars.

The forces of change in industry today are no less catastrophic than the effects of all the wars fought this century. Every continent is engaged, scrambling for field advantage. Every citizen is considered fodder for the campaign. All available resources are funneled into the organization's machine. Product output that is quick, cheap, and wanted is how generals will win the twenty-first century's economic war.

CHAPTER TWO

UNDERSTANDING OUR PERSONALITY STYLE

I speak at seminars and conferences all over the NAFTA region of the United States, Canada, and Mexico. What never ceases to amaze me is how Hippocrates' four behavioral styles consistently present themselves time after time, among my audiences. I present this information on differences in employee behavioral styles in an interactive format. My audiences are invited to participate by selecting one of the four behavioral styles which best describes them. Then, given a group assignment, the audiences naturally act out their different behavioral styles among the four different groups who are present at the seminar.

Describing Yourself Exercise

People's ability to understand themselves and others is critical to the increasingly competitive future we all face. Teams of people are required to survive this brutal global competition: people who can relate to, interact with, challenge and bring out the best in each other.

Target Systems

What follows is the written set of descriptions of the four behavioral styles from which you can now select the style that best suits you. In this exercise there are four sections, each of which has a list of 12 adjectives. Slowly read over the four sections and think carefully about yourself. Place check marks beside those adjectives that best describes you.

SECTION 1

I am best described as:

____ Risk-Taker	____ Organizer
____ Direct	____ Independent
____ Fast-Paced	____ Generalist
____ Self-Starting	____ Money-Motivated
____ Controlling	____ Free-Wheeling
____ Results-Oriented	____ Impatient

SECTION 2

I am best described as:

____ Charming	____ Outspoken
____ Variety	____ Excitable
____ Persuasive	____ Demanding
____ Enthusiastic	____ Competitive
____ People-Oriented	____ Colorful Dresser
____ Impatient	____ Promotes Self

SECTION 3

I am best described as:

____ Systematic	____ Mentor
____ Streamlines Steps	____ Patient Listener
____ Laid-Back	____ Routine-Oriented
____ Tolerant	____ Stubborn
____ Builds Trust	____ Coach
____ Fair	____ Networker

SECTION 4

I am best described as:

____ Perfectionistic	____ Precise Appearance
____ Cautious	____ Diplomatic
____ Emotionally Private	____ Thorough
____ Detailed	____ Persistent
____ Quality-Minded	____ Follow-Up
____ Judgmental	____ Rule-Oriented

When you have completed this adjective selection process, notice the one section that has more
check marks beside the adjectives than the other
three sections. Select the *One Section* of adjectives that has the most check marks as the one that
best describes you. Though you may believe you
could be any of the four sections, most people have
behavioral styles that match just one (or two) of
the sections, but not all four sections.

In each of the four sections, there is an in-
complete sentence: "I'm best described as . . . ."
In Section 1, complete the sentence, "I'm best
described as a TOP GUN." The STAR *icon*
corresponds with the Top Gun Hero. In Section
2, complete the sentence, "I'm best described as a
PALACE GUARD." The FLAG *icon* corresponds with the Palace Guard Hero. In Section
3, complete the sentence, "I'm best described as
INFANTRY." The BOOTS *icon* corresponds
with the Infantry war Hero. In Section 4, complete the sentence, "I'm best described as MILI-
TARY POLICE (MP)." The SCALES OF
JUSTICE *icon* corresponds with the MP war
Hero.

As you read the following basic Hero-style
descriptions, you may discover you resemble one
or two Hero-styles equally. For example, if you
are both an Infantry and Military Police (MP)
Hero, then read those chapters that relate to these
two Hero-styles.

In my experience with people, it is not un-
common that readers "see" themselves as two

Hero-styles. Working with thousands of audiences, I find Top Guns also have some Palace Guard in their behavioral styles. Infantry and the MP are also common pairings of Hero-styles. To use this book, read both sections that apply to you.

Follow the Icon: Identifying the Heroes

In Chapter Three, find the *icon* of the war Hero description that corresponds to the section you selected as best describing your behavioral style. For example, if you selected "I am best described as Infantry," then find the BOOTS *icon* in Chapter Three and read the introductory Infantry description. Chapters Four, Five, Six, and Seven will separately describe each war Hero-style, in-depth. All you have to do is follow the military *icon* that corresponds with your selected adjective section.

CHAPTER THREE

ENTER THE HEROES

Military Heroes by their actions in war easily personify Hippocrates' four personality characteristics. These four Heroes are easy to imagine, easy to draw cartoons about, and easy symbols from which to understand complex concepts such as one's personality traits.

Top Guns: High Flyers

Remember the movie Top Gun? Tom Cruise played the part perfectly, flying his plane as though he owned the sky. He outgunned, outmaneuvered, outflew the adversary with a confidence that all of us in the movie theater could feel. We counted on him to win. We knew he'd win. And he did!

Top Guns must be in control.

31

Obvious traits making up the Top Guns' workstyle can be defined as follows:

- Must be in control
- Can be generous to others if they get results
- Defy organizational charts and titles
- Want to be boss
- Challenge management's authority
- Must have authority to reach the "bottom line"
- Exceedingly competitive in sports and business
- Gravitate to having the biggest and the best
- Tend not to be team-oriented
- Like selling ideas and money
- Want to give orders rather than take them
- Most effective when left alone to accomplish goals
- Excellent ability to solve complex problems
- Little interest in routine details
- Fascinated by novel machines and new technology
- Conceptual thinkers
- Unaware of how strongly they come across to other people
- Say exactly what they mean
- May challenge leadership and lead office coup attempts

The leader must be able to produce a vision that leads to transformation of the organization. If the vision is to align the people of the organization in support of the vision's goal, then the leaders must appreciate the differences of workstyle among their people and adapt the message to be clearly understood by each style.

Target Systems

· Use a tough "shield" to protect their emotions

Top Guns are single minded: they want their results. The end justifies any means they would take to achieve their goal. Like Tom Cruise's control of the sky against any MIG, the Top Guns in businesses seek to control their work worlds. They like to outmaneuver and outgun everyone. Staying in control means everything to a Top Gun. They strive for positions of leadership and chafe under rules laid down by others. They are risk-takers who seek the advantage of flying high to gain a perspective that alludes those who are low flyers. From their high vantage point, Top Guns can see the strategic advantage and orchestrate the ground wars to beat the competition.

"From their high vantage point, Top Guns can see the strategic advantage and orchestrate the ground wars to beat the competition."

Palace Guards: Glory, Glory Hallelujah

Palace Guards seek the glory of the war's victory. Staging battles, displaying insignias and medals, engaging in marching bands, saluting flags, and regaling in the finery and trappings of war is what attracts Palace Guards. How

Palace Guards need people.

they appear, the image of power or success they project is what their war is all about.

Imagine the World War II competition waged by Britain's General Bernard L. Montgomery (Monty) against United States' General George S. Patton. "Monty," a Palace Guard, waged a personal contest as to who was to win first in the European war theater, he or George. The War Room—the array of lieutenants rushing around enormously beautiful, illuminated tables imbedded with strategy maps, or walls covered with bright maps—tracks the infantry's progress with coded miniature flags. This was the clean war, the pretty war, the exciting war, where everyone looked successful and felt important. This was the glorious war of the Palace Guards. The Palace Guards can best be described as follows:

"This was the clean war, the pretty war, the exciting war, where everyone looked successful and felt important. This was the glorious war of the Palace Guards."

- Natural image-makers
- People-oriented
- Use persuasion to get results
- Promoter of self
- Excellent first impressions
- Work well with ideas
- Marketer of self and others
- Strong communicators
- Need to be liked by others
- Fear boredom
- Take business issues personally
- Build teams
- Enjoy being with people of influence

· Prefer variety and excitement
· Have a large network of acquaintances
· Trendsetting in personal attire
· Use emotionalism as a defense

The Palace Guards know everyone who is important. "Whom you know is as important as what you know," is the basic tenet of Palace Guards. Looking the part, acting the part, but not taking part in the mundane, Palace Guards look successful to others. Easy conversationalists, these powerful warriors talk a good battle and enthrall everyone with their war stories. Not happy with understatements, Palace Guards embellish their experiences with colorful anecdotes that are crowd pleasers. These successful communicators recall the minutest details of their experiences just to entertain their listeners. Audiences love Palace Guards. They remind us of the glory that comes in winning the war.

The Infantry: The Loyal Foot Soldier

Enter the masses. It is the Infantry Heroes who slog it out in the workplace trenches. Persevering, methodical, and patient soldiers, the Top Guns and Palace Guards count on the Infantry to win their wars

Infantry need fairness.

for them! Without the Infantry, the Top Guns would have to go into mundane battles or the Palace Guards would have to wear dull uniforms designed for soldiers who crawl on their bellies over the dirty landscapes of war. The Infantry can best be described as follows:

- Lead from expertise
- Reach objectives systematically
- Prefer harmonious and fair work environments
- Prefer scheduled environments
- Provide patient leadership
- Tolerate others
- Can explode under unfair pressure
- Persevere with follow-through
- Like complex routines
- Dress for function rather than fashion
- Need time to respond to change
- Cautious risk-takers
- Patient mentors or coaches
- Tend to be pressed into leadership
- Have few enemies and a small circle of close friends
- Do not like to cause conflict
- Tend to be emotionally reserved
- Tend to be loyal to fair management
- Use resentments as a defense

"The Infrantry . . . persevere with follow-through."

The Infantry are those durable people who, given an assignment, follow through to the bitter end. They become *expert* hand-to-hand combatants. They make learning how to win wars their life's work. Infantry soldiers diligently practice their skills to be the best Infantry soldiers in their company. And, when Top Guns fall, it is often the expert Infantry soldier who picks up the fallen flag and leads the troops out of battle.

Thought of as uninspiring by the Palace Guards, the Infantry leaders instill trust in those who work for them. Patient, thorough, and tolerant of other soldiers, Infantry leaders and Infantry employees can move mountains, one shovel at a time!

"The Infantry make learning how to win wars their life's work."

MP's: You're Guilty

Everyone fears the MP's. But these misunderstood soldiers are the unsung Heroes of war. They protect lawbreaking soldiers from themselves and others, brook no-nonsense in barroom brawls, and bring everyone to justice despite the guilty's rank! These Heroes are sticklers for following the military code. Bend a written rule? *Never!* Stiffly adhering to the law, MP's would rather be right than happy. MP's can best be described as follows:

MP's need justice.

- Hold strong personal values as to "right and wrong"
- Believe unless it can be done right, it

37

should not be done
· Go by the book, especially "their" book
· Precise and highly procedural
· Display judicial leadership style
· Formal and reserved leaders
· Quality-oriented perfectionists
· Detail-oriented
· Procrastinate
· Find what is wrong before seeing what is right
· Work best with structure
· Like to know what to do, when to do it, and how to do it
· Itemize details and checklists
· Doublecheck everything for accuracy
· Use blame as a defense

If we are to move from being over-managed, we must understand how to work with people whose workstyles (their approach to work) are different from our own. The four behavioral styles are critical to this understanding and our ability to create our vision.

Target Systems

The MP's precise physical appearance broadcasts their rigid philosophy: Do it right the first time. With every button buttoned, every knot tied perfectly, these Heroes are noticeable in a crowd of soldiers because of their clean-cut appearances. These soldiers hate to be wrong and can easily make life hell for those soldiers who screw up. Break a rule and you are dead meat! The MP's are watching everyone for the slightest infraction. They love it when they can exercise their authority and throw even Top Guns behind bars.

"The MP's are watching everyone for the slightest infraction."

Considered wet blankets by many, it is the MP's, however, who will fight to the end for their convictions. When every other soldier has called it quits, it is the MP's who will be the lonely standard bearer of their company's flag.

"Clearly business is over-managed and underled." - Haas

What's Next

The following four chapters will define in-depth each individual behavioral style: the Top Gun, the Palace Guard, the Infantry, and the Military Police (MP). Just locate your style's *icon* and read the corresponding chapter that best describes you.

After you have read about yourself and your behavioral style, then go back to Chapter Two. By using the same adjective selection process you used to discover your behavioral style, you can discover the behavioral style of those individuals at work with whom you currently experience conflict.

This hypervigilance is focused on doing things right rather than focusing on "are we doing the right thing?" The former is concerned with efficiency, the latter with effectiveness.

Target Systems

Select adjectives that best describe the person at work as you experience that person, *today.* After you have marked all the adjectives that apply to this person, select one section that best describes this individual, overall. Locate the military *icon* that corresponds to the section you just chose. This section exemplifies your chosen individual's behavioral styles. Now, following the *icon* for that behavioral style, read the individual's corresponding chapter.

This additional step of identifying the behavioral styles of those individuals with whom you

"Increasing your interpersonal skills in dealing with work conflicts comes from you understanding what makes you and your employees or work-colleagues 'tick'."

work and experience conflict will help you gain insight into their behavior. Therefore, you can understand what they need from you to decrease the conflicts you are experiencing with them.

In the place of conflict, you can now work to increase the quality of your work relationships. Increasing your interpersonal skills in dealing with work conflicts comes from you understanding what makes you and your employees or work-colleagues "tick." Greater self-knowledge and greater interpersonal knowledge between all managers and employees will reduce the civil wars now occurring in American organizations.

CHAPTER FOUR

THE TOP GUN'S CIVIL WAR

Most business enterprise is led by managers who give little thought to understanding their "Heroes," the employees who are engaged in creating the company's out-

put. Jobs are created and filled with new employees. Head honchos then expect everyone to produce. Even in instances when companies are forcibly merged with other companies or when departments of employees are reengineered for greater efficiency, employees are expected to be productive at the outset.

Little attention is paid to employees' personality traits by managers. Because of this, it is a constant miracle to me that anything is accomplished in the American workplace. Research studies have shown that most employees report they could work harder for their employers, but elect not to. What causes this underproductivity?

Wars by their nature are created from difference. A lasting and fruitful peace comes from understanding where we are the same and appreciating where we are different.

Target Systems

"Research studies have shown that most employees report they could work harder for their employers, but elect not to."

I believe the lack of employee industriousness could be a symptom of management's lack of knowledge of or disregard for their employees' personality differences. If managers do not recognize their employees' behavior styles (their Hero-style), it follows managers will also not understand how to structure work assignments for their employees, nor will they know how to motivate each of their employees for greater productivity and job satisfaction. These essential job enhancing factors, when missing, lead to employee job dissatisfaction, conflict, and poor job performance.

When misunderstood at work, all of our "Heroes," the Top Guns, Palace Guards, Infantry, and MP's, can perform badly. Top Guns will become a challenge to management, Palace Guards will become manipulative and overspend budgets, the Infantry will become a roadblock to progress, and MP's will blame everyone for not getting the job done.

"Where company mergers or downsizings occur throwing workforces together that have no shared work history, the stage is set for employee misunderstandings, fear, distrust, and conflict."

Where company mergers or downsizings occur throwing workforces together that have no shared work history, the stage is set for employee misunderstandings, fear, distrust, and conflict. These are the destructive dynamics that I describe as the American workplace civil war.

Misunderstood, employees become combatants and war with each other. Turf wars ensue. Back-stabbing is common. Dirty little rumors circulate to demoralize the "troops." New alliances galvanize individuals into warring parties to fight against the "enemy": management.

THE BATTLEFIELD:
High-Ticket Retail Store

THE COMBATANTS:
*Top Gun Boss and
Infantry Middle
Manager*

In a fast-action retail chain, John, the director of stores, was serving a customer on a $50,000 purchase when he heard his boss shouting from the other end of the 80,000 square foot showroom. As he divided his attention nervously from his customer's questions and his boss's shouting, John realized his boss, Franklin, was shouting for him!

"John, John! Where is that SOB?" John, use to Franklin's outbursts, continued to be attentive to his customer until Franklin was coming down the next aisle. In a low-keyed voice John replied, "Franklin, I'd like you to meet our customer, Mr. Price." Franklin, not to be deterred by a customer standing in front of him bellowed, "Some SOB is standing in my warehouse saying you'd told him he could return his purchase! Did you tell that SOB he could return his merchandise?"

John, recollecting the customer well, stated "Yes, Franklin, I did. The merchandise was defective and I told him, in all fairness, to return it for a refund or replacement."

Franklin turned purple! "G--D---it, John, you know I don't allow customers to return merchandise. Now, you get back there and tell that

It is becoming apparent that companies who have downsized or focused on cost-cutting have not done as well as those who have utilized employees individually and in groups to create a new or different organization and methods to add value in solutions to customers' needs.

Target Systems

43

SOB he's to take his stuff back out of my warehouse and get the hell out of my store!"

John, ever an Infantry soldier, maintained his calm *and* his ground. In a patient voice he said, "I could do that Franklin, but my customer, Mr. Price, is very interested in buying our $50,000 package. Would you like me to stay here and finish writing up his ticket or would you prefer I go to the warehouse?"

Franklin, hearing the fifty grand, immediately got his Top Gun priorities straight. "No, no, you stay here with Mr. Price. I'll handle that SOB in the warehouse." Promptly Franklin went to the phone, called the police, *and had his customer in the warehouse arrested!*

To end this story, John eventually left this company; not because he was not doing the job. John left because Franklin's Top Gun leadership style crushed John's Infantry need to play fair with his customer. Who lost this war? Everyone, including Franklin's customer.

"John left because Franklin's Top Gun leadership style crushed John's Infantry need to play fair."

Funny Thing About Wars

Though this real life story is entertaining (the names were changed to protect identities), Franklin looked high and low for someone like John to hire as director of stores. He wanted someone who could follow his store's systems, who was highly

knowledgeable and "good with customers." John
was that Infantry man!

In turn, John was excited about Franklin
pursuing him for the store's opportunity. John was
interested in having a strong, Top Gun leader. He
liked someone crusty who could make the tough
decisions and lead employees through the thick
and thin of retail. He *liked* Franklin! Franklin
respected John. Then, what happened to cause
these two Heroes to fail as employer and employee?

Franklin lacked the knowledge of how to effectively manage John for results. Like most Top
Guns, Franklin believed everyone could become a
Top Gun, just by talking louder! Franklin swore
in his heart-of-hearts John wanted to be a Top Gun
too, like Franklin.

The funny part of this war story is that John,
unaware of his Infantry style, sought yet another
Top Gun to work for. He *needs* a Top Gun boss.
And, Franklin? Well, Franklin hired yet another
Infantry soldier as his new director of stores.
However, this time, Franklin conferred with me
and became aware of the new director of stores'
personality style. I warned Franklin, "Your new
director of stores *must have a sense of fair play*, or
he'll quit."

Can Franklin alter his Top Gun approach
when necessary to meet the needs of his newest
Infantry warrior, his director of stores? Only time
will tell. For his newest director of stores to stay
and be productive will require that Franklin (and

"Like most Top Guns, Franklin believed everyone could become a Top Gun, just by talking louder!"

the rest of the family management) acts purposefully rather than explosively. Franklin must slow his impatience and see the world as his new director of stores sees the world. That's Franklin's job: Inspire his troops to conquer higher grounds.

THE BATTLEFIELD:
Retail Stores
THE COMBATANTS:
Top Gun Salesperson and the Customer

"Top Guns are attracted to ownership and entrepreneurialism." This style often leads to under appreciation of the needs of the other styles.

Target Systems

Top Guns are attracted to ownership and entrepreneurialism. Though they may begin their careers in other organizations, Top Guns chafe when controlled by others. I have found many Top Guns on retail sales floors in companies owned by second-generation owners (who are often Infantry Heroes, *unlike* their Top Gun founding parent). Top Gun salespeople love working under Infantry bosses! Why? Because Infantry bosses love keeping people happy!

How are Top Guns kept happy? By giving them opportunities to make a lot of money on their own terms. Because of management's advertising efforts, retail sales offer them all of these terms— lots of freedom and lots of ready-made customers for them to cash in on. In inside sales, Top Gun salespeople pick and choose which customers they wait on. And, what types of customers do Top Guns love to wait on? Customers who have already decided to buy. All they need is someone to write up their purchase ticket. Enter the Top Guns! After passing off the customers' paperwork to be completed by the "helpful" Infantry or MP office clerk, Top Guns now collect a good commission, which is happily paid by the Infantry boss.

Everyone is happy! Right? Wrong! What happened to the customer?

"How are Top Guns kept happy? By giving them opportunities to make a lot of money on their own terms."

Customer Surveys

National surveys of retail customers continually report customers' dissatisfaction with the quality of sales help. They report, "the salesperson wasn't interested in me" or "the salesperson didn't seem to care about me."

Top Guns *can be caring*. But, they need to be paid for it!

"National surveys of retail customers continually report customers' dissatisfaction with the quality of sales help."

THE BATTLEFIELD:
    Small Southwestern Retail Store
THE COMBATANTS:
    Top Gun Salesperson and His Customer

Harry is a successful salesperson in a small retail store located in a small town. Everyone knows almost everyone else, unless a new family moves to town. These newcomers are quickly assimilated by the townsfolk, including our salesperson, Harry. What does a move into a new home automatically require of its new owners? That they buy more or different home furnishings. Happily, for Harry, he sells home furnishings!

Mr. Jones, a newcomer, came into Harry's store needing to buy an entire bedroom suite for his new home. This newcomer represented a good sale for Harry. In a commanding manner, Harry immediately took Mr. Jones to the store's most expensive line, even though Harry didn't take time to ask Mr. Jones what budget he had in mind for his purchase.

The trouble with Top Gun salespeople is they are interested in getting their own commission needs met. As a result, they tend to ask few questions of their customers, as this "only slows the sale." They tend to present to their customers those items that will give the salesperson the biggest commission. After selecting a lovely bedroom suite, Mr. Jones complained about the $5,000 price tag and attempted to negotiate the price with Harry. Harry knew Mr. Jones wanted that particular set of furniture and was not about to lower his price. But, Mr. Jones stood his ground and this upset Harry. Harry's impatience with Mr. Jones soon took over. When Mr. Jones would not relent on the $5,000 price tag, but insisted he still wanted to buy the furniture, Harry exploded, "You SOB! Get out of this store, NOW!" and promptly threw Mr. Jones out the door.

End of story? NOT. Mr. Jones meekly came back into the store and bought his bedroom suite, for $5,000. Harry felt *wonderful!*

Harry got his sale today, but he may have lost another $50,000 in lifelong sales to Mr. Jones and his family. Harry loses sight of these things in the glory of collecting his fat commission on today's Mr. Jones's bedroom sale. And, Harry doesn't worry about losing Mr. Jones as a long-term customer. Why? Harry's Infantry boss will continue to pay +6 percent of all sales revenue in advertising costs to continually bring NEW customers to Harry. This keeps Harry happy, which in turn keeps Harry's boss happy.

"Harry got his sale today, but he may have lost another $50,000 in lifelong sales."

This real life story of customer abuse (names changed to protect identity) is repeated daily in every retail store in the country. Maybe not as violent as throwing customers out the door, but it's no wonder national retail customer surveys continue to find customers upset with salespeople. The cost of customer abuse to the retail industry is monumental. Lower overall sales, poor close ratios, and fewer repeat customers are the result of Top Guns approach to selling to their retail customers. The hard fact in furniture retail is that over 15,000 stores have closed their doors permanently since 1991. This represents a loss of almost 50 percent of traditional furniture retail stores.

"The cost of customer abuse to the retail industry is monumental."

Is this all because of Harry and other Top Gun salespeople? No.

Our Infantry retail bosses are as much at fault because of their tolerance for the Top Gun's poor sales performance. This results in higher labor costs and lower returns on the store's advertising dollars. It all adds up to retail stores losing money rather than making it, and retail customers are getting ready to stop being abused by retail salespeople. How? By buying from the privacy of their own homes through using customer-friendly catalogs, shopping the electronic "malls" found in cyberspace, or buying from the likes of QVC television channels. Are Top Guns able to change their behaviors to suit the demands made on them in their workplace? Only when they are given hard choices such as change or going to work for someone else. Unfortunately, many Top Guns leave rather than change. What do they often do for their next job? They start their own businesses!

Founders and Entrepreneurs

I have been profiling founding fathers and mothers, people who started their own companies, since the 1970s and over 99 percent are Top Guns. This finding is astounding, considering the many industries and people I have worked with. Being a Top Gun is a prerequisite for successful entrepreneurialism, no matter what the business or enterprise. Top Guns are our risk-takers and entrepreneurs. Finding it difficult to work under many organizational constraints, Top Guns have such faith in their own abilities to make money that it is not difficult for them to quit jobs and strike out on their own.

"Being a Top Gun is a prerequisite for successful entrepreneurialism."

Top Guns keep their eye on horizons, looking for opportunities and ways to take advantage of circumstance. Ray Krok, the founder of McDonald's, is such an example. A Top Gun, he realized the McDonald brothers had created a wonderful opportunity for him. These Infantry-type brothers had systematized making hamburgers to such a fine art that every hamburger was consistently as good as their last or their next one.

With the McDonald brothers' penchant for systems and Ray's Top Gun penchant for capitalizing on an opportunity, this partnership was bound to be a success. In the early 1950s with more mothers working outside the home, the country was looking for a quick, cheap, and tasty alternative to home cooking. With McDonald's, we all found a *reliable* and inexpensive eating experience that we trusted week after week. And, McDonald's became the household word for fast food the world over.

"With the McDonald brothers' penchant for systems and Ray's Top Gun penchant for capitalizing on an opportunity, this partnership was bound to be a success."

CHAPTER FIVE

THE PALACE GUARD'S CIVIL WAR

Being and remaining successful in business requires leaders
to be sensitive to and responsible for a diverse workforce.
Without psychologically aware
leadership, many employees
lose faith and trust in their employers. Treated
too harshly, as a number or as a machine, many
former employees have "snapped," visiting violence
on their workplaces.

"Without psychologi-
cally aware leader-
ship, many employ-
ees lose faith and trust
in their employers."

This civil war carnage will continue. Organizations have not yet become profitable enough
to stop the merging and dejobbing of America's
workplace. Permanent job loss continues, especially among middle management, technical, and
many professional positions. IBM, Kodak, General Dynamics, Boeing, General Electric, John
Deere, General Motors, Nabisco, Ford, and
AT&T have led the country in stunning job cuts
in the final decades of the twentieth century.

53

"Since 1973, personal income has decreased 20 percent."

Service industry jobs, however, continue to show promise as their hiring projections increase. The tough reality of this job shift is that jobs being lost and jobs replacing them are not comparable in pay scale. Since 1973, personal income has decreased 20 percent. Jobs that paid $8.55 per hour in 1973, now pay just $7.54.

The view between the business and employment prognosticators continues to hold that people will work longer hours for fewer dollars. This is especially true in the service industries.

The pay scale in service jobs is significantly less than the pay scale of the lost white collar jobs. Even now millions of families toil long hours in service-related jobs and barely meet poverty level incomes. There is something wrong when people work more than 40 hours a week and remain below federal poverty guidelines. Increases in part-time jobs and people taking multiple jobs are signals of companies searching for ways to reduce labor costs, including employee benefits. That these shifts are continuing, presents a dark future for many middle- and low-income American families.

"Increases in part-time jobs and people taking multiple jobs are signals of companies searching for ways to reduce labor costs."

When Will It End?

The spectre of global competition continues to pit American employers against their employees as companies try to cope with world economic pres-

sures. Business leaders are scrambling to keep
their corporate "heads" afloat as their organizations are economically threatened from across the
seas. The Pacific Rim, the European community, and the emergence of China are formidable
economic competitors for the American dollar and
the customer.

"American employers try to cope with world economic pressures."

These newly organized global economies are
"blessed" with a flood of workers who are willing
to work for pennies compared to the average pay
of the American wage earner. Significantly low
labor costs, abundance of resources coupled with
these emerging foreign companies' ability to manu-
facture high-quality "clones" of products in such
powerful American industries as electronics and
high-tech computer hardware and software, will
force American businesses to continue to struggle
to define "employment" to their employees. The
frustrating realization is that the rupturous job shifts
occurring in American businesses today will continue. The world economy is in the throes of re-
definition, and American business will be fortunate just to maintain an economic edge into the
twenty-first century.

"American business will be fortunate just to maintain an economic edge into the twenty-first century."

Enter the Palace Guards

Who can make the best of an
awful situation? Our Palace

Guards! Ever confident in their ability to win opportunities and impress people, Palace Guards are
masters at marketing themselves. Palace Guards
like themselves. Optimists, they are confident of
their abilities to "sell themselves" to the power
brokers. Easy conversationalists, they initially put
almost everyone at ease. Palace Guards *look successful*, even when they are down to their last dime.

I recall a national television news program
that covered a woman, a Palace Guard, who was
discovered living out of her car in Hollywood,
California. Her wealthy husband had divorced
her in a sudden, shocking, and swift decision. Having no marketable skills, this former homemaker
was bereft of maintaining her standard of living.

As a Palace Guard, she valued her former
social status in her community, going to work for
an hourly wage seemed unthinkable. So she set
up a life out of her automobile that gave her the
appearance of status. Still a fashion plate, she wore
clothes that were now packed in boxes in the car's
back seat. During the news program's interview,
her style was that of a gracious host just out for an
afternoon stroll. She washed in anonymous con-
venience stores and gas stations. She got her
makeup and nails done by setting appointments
at the local department stores where it was done
as a "free trial." To accept charity was out of the
question. It did not fit her self-image.

Palace Guards are *image-makers*. They
know looking successful is just a step away from
being successful. Palace Guards like to drive the

best cars, live in the best locations, wear the newest fashions, and can be name droppers, as ways to market their success image. No matter the audience, Palace Guards are sure to hold the center stage.

Infantry soldiers love Palace Guards; Top Guns are impressed with the Palace Guard's glib conversational style, especially if the Palace Guard knows what he or she is talking about. The MP's are not so generous. Natural skeptics, MP's wait for the Palace Guard to make mistakes. MP's are not impressed with the Palace Guard's penchant for exaggerations. They believe Palace Guards are "windbags" due to their love of talking on and on. However, a break for Palace Guards, MP's are seldom quick to publically voice their doubts of Palace Guards, for fear of being wrong.

The Palace Guard's Civil War

THE BATTLEFIELD:
   R.J. Reynolds—
   Nabisco
THE COMBATANT:
   Ross Johnson, CEO

Perhaps no greater example of a Palace Guard exists than Ross Johnson, former head of R.J. Reynolds (RJR) and Nabisco. Producing his image as a successful CEO became a heavy expense to the company's bottom line according to the book, *Barbarians at the Gate*. Ross's expenses were reportedly so extensive that one RJR-Nabisco insider predicted the company could see substantial growth in their operating income, simply by cutting Ross's image-enhancing spending structures. There was a fleet of 10 corporate jets, housed in a private $12 million Atlanta hangar built especially for the jet fleet, that was at Johnson's management team's disposal. Once there was a mysterious passenger listed as simply G. Shepherd on a flight's passenger manifest. Insiders claim this was Ross's dog, Rocco, though Ross denies the flight was for the purpose of transporting Rocco back to Winston-Salem.

Ross surrounded himself with famous people. Golfers, entertainers, and others were retained for a fee up to $1 million a year just to mingle with Ross's party guests. Ross would give away Gucci watches at corporate parties and became incensed when a local newspaper reported he gave $50 tips. He was angry because he hadn't tipped anyone as low as $50 in years. Ross charmed everyone he met in every set of circumstances. For those working with him, he gave them unlimited expense accounts, corporate apartments, and unlimited use of the corporate jet fleet. His leadership team would meet at all times of the night, mixing pleasure and work into the wee hours. The next day, people would return to the office when they could. During the Ross Johnson years, RJR-Nabisco was an exciting place to work.

Palace Guards like Ross Johnson love excitement. Demoralized by routine operational details, Ross would regularly reorganize departments just for the fun of it. His method of management was referred to as "shit stirring." If things got too boring, change it! Palace Guards fear being "killed" by boredom. Innovation is an up-side result of Palace Guards running from boredom. However, disastrous lack of attention to bottom-line details is the downside of Palace Guards' avoidance of routine.

A man perhaps ahead of his time, Ross, in his need for change, created the work concept of assignments rather than jobs. In the assignment concept, people are placed or hired to complete assignments rather than spend 40 hours a week at a full-time job. Today's approach to the current paradigm job shift in the American workplace is temporary projects or work assignments. Part-time work is replacing full-time jobs as a way to lower labor costs. Fortune magazine referred to this phenomena as the "Dejobbing of America." Adopting the most flexible of workstyles, Palace Guards, like the proverbial cat, can always land on their feet. When Ross was deposed at RJR-Nabisco in an aborted LBO, he left with a $53 million severance package.

Palace Guards are inspiring. We love them for their ability to entertain us and make us laugh or give us a sense of belonging. Team-builders, Palace Guards attract other strong people to work for them. They love other Palace Guards!

"Innovation is an up-side result of Palace Guards running from boredom."

"A man perhaps ahead of his time, Ross, in his need for change, created the work concept of assignments rather than jobs."

Temporary projects or work assignments are replacing full-time jobs.

Target Systems

59

At one of our client companies, a well-known national industry journal, the staff was initially 100 percent Palace Guards. Without knowing why, the Palace Guard hiring managers were instinctively attracted to applicants who were also Palace Guards. By virtue of being a Palace Guard, the applicant had a ticket into the company.

The magazine is an exciting place to work. Meeting lots of industry personalities, writing about them, and showcasing the staff at national shows all meets the needs of these Palace Guards. The magazine's head honcho is an outrageously wonderful Palace Guard. The first time I met her she breezed by me at top speed during a national show, singing, "I love your services. I'll get back to you soon!" I had never seen this person before, but she talked to me as though she was an ardent fan! That's what Palace Guards do. They make others feel wonderful.

"That's what Palace Guards do. They make others feel wonderful."

Palace Guards Are in the Business of People

Palace Guards focus their efforts on influencing others to do their bidding. Whether it is sales, management, marketing, or finance, Palace Guards always build relationships with people. A Palace Guard being in a job that does not include public contact is like placing an orchid in the desert. They will wilt and die of boredom. Instead, these individuals feed on the excitement of the moment in which they win someone over, attract a new client, or make a high-ticket sale.

"A Palace Guard being in a job that does not include public contact is like placing an orchid in the desert."

Avant-garde, Palace Guards can be shocking to non-Palace Guards. Cutting-edge fashion, preferring extravagant offices, often outspoken and seeking to be the center of attention, these Palace Guards can never be ignored.

In one of our retail client's store, a next generation son of a Top Gun founder is a Palace Guard. In an attempt to bring excitement and the unusual to spice up the store, the son brought his pot-bellied pig, Molly, to work. The local television news station picked up the story and our young Palace Guard and "Molly" were on TV. They loved it!

It was an exciting image-maker in the eyes of this young man. Something unique. Was his Top Gun father impressed? NOT! In his eyes, he wanted to know how having Molly, the pot-bellied pig, on television was going to increase sales.

How can Palace Guards use their penchant for the unusual to make the difference between producing business and losing business? Learning to focus on bottom-line results rather than just creating excitement is an excellent starting place. Management setting realistic goals, demanding performance deadlines, and well-defined budgets

"Management setting realistic goals, demanding performance deadlines, and well-defined budgets all help Palace Guards remain focused on business."

all help Palace Guards remain focused on business. Public praise for a job well done also enhances a Palace Guard's drive to perform.

Listening to others rather than "holding court" is another skill that increases a Palace Guard's effectiveness. Without the ability to actively listen to others, Palace Guards' ability to perform is seriously impeded. Poor with time management, known for holding long meetings in which the Palace Guard hogs the floor, and intensely emotional, these individuals can quickly turn a workplace into high drama. All this reduces a staff's focus on getting results and serving their customers. If Palace Guards need us to like them, what causes them not to be good listeners? The lack of listening skills appears to be rooted in the Palace Guards' intense personal focus on getting their needs met through other people. They need for you to like them. They entertain you in hopes of you liking them in return. Without your approval, these individuals tend to become demoralized and even moody. They easily lose their objectivity and personalize work issues.

"I didn't get the account because they didn't like me."

"I didn't get the account because they didn't like me" is a common belief among Palace Guards. Once when working with a large financial organization's outside sales staff, I found a wonderful Palace Guard who had great

difficulty making cold calls. When the company bought our rapport-building cold calling sales system, this young man wailed, "You mean I have to go back to that agent even if she doesn't like me?" This salesperson equated making sales with his first step, that of making friends. With this subjective approach, his rate of closings was well below those of other salespeople on staff. He needed to learn objectivity and customer-focus rather than turning sales calls into social calls.

 We need Palace Guards. Without them, the fresh ideas, the spontaneity, the outrageous antics that keep a workforce light and innovative are missing. In one client company headed by an MP, he had a basic distrust of the glib Palace Guard types. Instead, he preferred the serious, durable, passive, head-down, and work-type Heroes such as the Infantry and MP's like himself. However, this company served other companies and in this role was responsible for staging social events of vast magnitude. Now, I ask you, would you invite an MP or a Palace Guard to *your* party?

Our first assignment with this organization was to help the MP-CEO hire people who could create exciting events for their national clients. We hired Palace Guards to stage the events and to attend them as well. We hired Infantry to work in

"Now, I ask you, would you invite an MP or a Palace Guard to your party?"

the offices, to follow through on all the routine, service-related customer contacts, and MP's to make sure everyone did their jobs right. Through a balance of workstyles, this staff is now attracting attention from other major industries, seeking help with their national shows. This is the basic principle from which we operate: match a person's workstyle to the job. If you want excitement, hire Palace Guards. If you want quality work turned out every time, hire MP's. If you want your customers to have patient, friendly, routine follow-up, hire the Infantry.

By matching workstyles of people to the work you want done, you can enjoy lowered employee turnover and increased bottom-line productivity.

However, you must know what a job requires before you can select the correct workstyle. For example, my first research project upon entering the consulting world was to find "good salespeople" for our many retail clients. Since I had never sold much retail other than high-ticket lingerie when I was a freshman at the university, I had no idea what workstyle was best-suited for other types of retail sales.

"I found the Infantry rather than the Palace Guard to be the most common workstyle serving retail customers."

From my original descriptive research, for example, I found the Infantry rather than the Palace Guard to be the most common workstyle serving retail customers. Surprised? So was everyone else! Since that early research, the Infantry salesperson tends to predominate in retail.

It is not difficult for managers to be attracted to and want to hire the exciting, dynamic, smooth talking Palace Guards. They energize the sales floor. And, if organizations provide them powerful incentives to produce, these warriors can be amazing sales performers. They will require objective management, someone who can hold their Palace Guard's attention to bottom-line results using proper channels or policies as established by the company. Without dispassionate management, Palace Guards become hotbeds of emotionalism and demanding prima donnas that demoralize everyone involved.

> *"They will require objective management, someone who can hold their Palace Guard's attention to bottom-line results."*

Winners and Cheerleaders

Our Palace Guards are true marketers. They know the value of image-making. These Heroes can verbally paint a picture of success from the ashes of previous ruin. Opportunists, no one believes in Palace Guards quite like themselves. They are sublime at influencing other people and often drafted by their teammates to represent them to the power brokers. Excellent at establishing initial rapport, Palace Guards can win the account, win hearts of both employee and client and influence opinions better than any of the four Heroes.

CHAPTER SIX

THE INFANTRY'S CIVIL WAR

Over many years I have pro-
filed and observed profiles of
more than 50,000 individuals.
In all those cases, I have found
only five Infantry warriors who
founded their own companies.

However, of those five Infantry founders, only two
businesses resulted. It took three of these Infantry
soldiers to start one business and two to start the
other. Obvious in my sample population, Infantry warriors are not known for their
entrepreneurialism. To start a business requires
taking a risk. Infantry Heroes are not fond of risks.
They schedule their lives in a way to avoid them
at all cost. Instead, Infantry leaders are often found
as second, third, or fourth generation owners. They
can expertly maintain a business once it is con-
structed by a Top Gun. Eager to learn the business, Infantry managers become exceedingly pro-
ficient in gaining industry-related knowledge.
Once experts, Infantry leaders are known for their

*"Infantry leaders are
often found as sec-
ond, third, or fourth
generation owners."*

ability to create trust among those employees who report to them.

Patient, tolerant, and happiest when helping others, Infantry leaders make excellent mediators and mentors. Their grasp of their industries, their knowledge about the company's product(s), and their strong customer base can make these leaders highly valuable to their organizations. However, Infantry leaders fear of controversy is their greatest leadership liability.

An Infantry Educator's Civil War

THE BATTLEFIELD:
 Harvard University
THE COMBATANT:
 Harvard President

In The Wall Street Journal, the description of Harvard University's newest president fits the Infantry leader. Hired to unify the many independent and entrepreneurial academic schools that make up Harvard, this president began to make strides in bringing all 13 schools and its deans under one academic roof.

However, when budget cuts threatened to reduce benefits, the conciliatory tone of the college deans took a cold turn. Outraged at the president's proposed cutbacks, they rose as one to oppose him. Vocal, loud, and attacking, the deans took out after their new president.

After one such meeting, it was later reported the president, in a manner unlike him, became "brusque" and left the meeting. Later, the newspapers reported the president, due to exhaustion from working 120 hour weeks, had not been seen for several weeks.

What brought the new president to such exhaustion is also the strife and conflict that followed once he began to move to seriously unify Harvard. Infantry Heroes abhor conflict. Instead, they spend their lives attempting to bring harmony to all. Peacekeepers, they often say "Yes" when they feel "No." They endure endless routines, faithfully following through on what is expected. Will Harvard's new president survive his civil war? The latest report is he'll return this spring and his Board of Directors vow to "help him." The battle continues.

The Challenge of Change

Following established guidelines, Infantry warriors are like ducks out of water when faced with sudden controversy brought on by change. During industry shifts, when faced with new competitors or cost-saving innovative approaches, Infantry lead-

"Unwilling to risk what has been their gain, Infantry leaders first play it safe."

ers waddle to a stop. Unwilling to risk what has been their gain, Infantry leaders first play it safe. They would rather keep the peace than take risks that only "might" reduce costs or increase profits.

Infantry leaders can be doomsday leaders. With change, they fear the worst rather than seek new fortunes. As a result, second generation leaders often miss valuable business opportunities, so strong is their belief that what they already have is more valuable. Since many company founders tend to be Top Guns, when second generation Infantry leaders take over the helm, they are reluctant to alter their founders' course. Companies miss new opportunities and become museums of their founders. "Dad always did it this way," and dutifully, so does the son or daughter.

Transformation

"In their efforts to keep everyone happy, our two Infantry leaders became emotional shells."

In another client organization, we began work with the third generation Infantry son. His second generation Infantry father was still very active in the stores. This high-end retail chain attracted many Palace Guards to work for them. As the chain grew, so did the organizational conflict. To get their own way, the Palace Guards emotionally intimidated the owners. In their efforts to keep everyone happy, our two Infantry leaders became emotional shells. By keeping the peace, they had lost the war to their highly dramatic Palace Guards. The help was now running the business. Depressed, anxious, and possibly alcoholic, the father had given the challenge of running the business over to his son. The son was in no better shape than the father. His model for leadership resembled his dad's.

Keep the peace at any cost. And the cost in psychological distress for these two Infantry leaders was enormous. The son displayed no emotion, rarely smiled, and was a ghost of a man. In our Leadership Training, he appeared uninspired and meek, but attentive. His fellow leaders/students were mostly Top Guns and after kissing this Infantry leader off as a loser, proceeded to act as though he did not exist in the classroom.

"Keep the peace at any cost."

However, by the fourth day of training, our Infantry leader had gained some ground. He'd watched repeatedly as the Top Guns attempted to resolve challenging employee issues. Though their challenges were different from his, our Infantry leader began to show signs of life. His strong knowledge of the industry, his thorough diligence in assessing the value of change finally paid off.

During a class exercise, a particularly powerful Top Gun wrestled with his attempts to roleplay his loss of control over a highly dramatic Palace Guard employee. She was highly emotional and confrontive, and it was apparent to all in the room this Top Gun had been bested by this employee. After a particularly tough exchange, the Top Gun sat back in his chair, emotionally exhausted by his role-play struggle to regain control of his Palace Guard. In the silence that broke over the group, a quiet Infantry voice said: "Shoot her."

Our Infantry leader lived! The roof blew off the training room with the Top Guns' thundering applause and shouts of approval. Our Infantry leader gained stature in the eyes of his powerful peers and with himself. We now call him "The Shooter" and he grins from ear to ear. This Infantry leader is in transformation. He may win the civil war in his organization.

Yet, his battle continues.

Victim or Volunteer?

Unfortunately, the Infantry can believe they fall victim to the people they attempt to manage. Unable to naturally take an aggressive stand, Infantry leaders give ground to the Top Guns and Palace Guards that work for them. Surrendering the reins of leadership, the Infantry wonder what happened to their wonderful plans for workplace harmony.

Facing Infantry leaders grappling with an organization in which they *gave up* control, the first myth I dispel is that they are victims of their circumstances. I point out Infantry leaders' natu-

72

ral tendencies to kill their employees with kindness. When that doesn't work and the company civil wars continue, Infantry leaders seek shelter in their offices and operational tasks.

As if they are fulfilling some kind of peace treaty, the Infantry leaders begin to do the work of their employees rather than start a war. When I find an Infantry leader working in the "trenches" of the organization, I know I am looking at a leader who believes he or she has been taken prisoner.

NONSENSE! I am famous for my statement to all Infantry leaders: There are no victims after the age of 18, only volunteers. If you don't like what is happening in your organization, *change it!* Compliance and avoidance of civil war only encourage escalation of employee rebellion. All employees require leadership. When Infantry leaders abdicate their leadership roles, the ensuing loss of authority invites war. The Top Guns will take over; the Palace Guards will create high drama as they scramble for their share of the booty. The Infantry become entrenched.

The MP's become hostile and bitter toward everyone. Judgmental, our military police find fault with everyone even on good days. When leaders encourage others to lead themselves, anarchy reins. This is an MP's greatest fear. With no one in charge, everyone stands the chance of being hurt.

With 85 percent of all companies failing under second generation leadership, a part of this failure rate is, in my experience, due to ineffectual, peace-keeping Infantry leadership. In an attempt

"Compliance and avoidance of civil war only encourage escalation of employee rebellion."

"When leaders encourage others to lead themselves, anarchy reins."

73

to maintain the status quo of their Top Gun founders, the Infantry's reluctance to embrace needed change and their peace-keeping approach to employee management are what finally destroys the next generations' Infantry owners' organizations. Our employees need leaders. When Infantry second generation leaders learn to take risks, to accept conflict as a natural extension of the workplace, and to innovate when competition demands, only then will they realize their true rewards: peace and continued prosperity.

THE BATTLEFIELD:
Financial Sales Organization
THE COMBATANTS:
Infantry Boss and Top Gun Financial Sales Force

A client company headed by an Infantry owner contacted us to resolve low sales results within his financial sales force. After profiling all of the salespeople, it was apparent one of the main issues facing the owner was his Top Gun sales force. These men (and a woman) rejected any attempts by the Infantry owner to manage their performances. Fiercely independent, Top Guns fought turf wars, completely ignoring any concept such as sales territories. Any potential customer was fresh meat for the Top Guns. Demanding, intimidating, and controlling, the Top Guns had the Infantry owner cowered in the corner of his own organization. What did the Infantry owner do to rectify his dilemma? He paid them more money, gave them bigger cuts of the pie, and even let his Top Guns negotiate points with the company's lenders.

The owner paid for training, paid for leads, paid for gifts to customers and potential customers, took his Top Guns on lavish trips and then wondered why his return on investment was not paying handsomely. His last straw was when he realized, in looking over his P&L, that his Top Gun salespeople were being paid more than the owner paid himself.

Where did he go wrong? What could he do to fix his tenuous financial situation? These were questions he asked pleadingly, hoping we could come in and straighten up his Top Guns. The Infantry owner wanted us to rescue him, as though he was a victim of his employees.

NONSENSE!

Our first step in advising our Infantry owner was to have him agree to develop an organizational plan for his company. Strategic planning, setting corporate goals, proper staffing, lowering labor costs, and establishing personal sales goals for every salesperson culminated our initial work. From there, the Infantry owner had to communicate to his Top Guns that they worked for him, not the other way around. He dropped the many perks he'd previously provided the sales force. These were now expected to be paid by the Top Guns,

"The Infantry owner had to communicate to his Top Guns that they worked for him, not the other way around."

out of their expenses and/or commissions (which remained healthy). Any customer they brought to the company was expected to maximize the company's health, not just line the satin pockets of the highly paid Top Guns. And, the results of these moves?

The Infantry owner's worst fear was realized. His top four producers left, taking key-administrative staff members with them. It was this fear of staff abandonment in the heat of the battle that had kept the Infantry owner paying huge ransoms to his financial sales force. He had fantasied the Top Gun walkout as a death stroke to his organization. No one would come to work for him after that and he'd have a dying company. Sales would dry up and in the end, the Infantry owner believed he'd be living in poverty.

"Our Infantry owner's company became a mecca for salespeople seeking a fine opportunity."

However, it was because he was compliant and subservient to his employees that the Infantry owner almost shot his own organization's chances for survival. He was the problem in his company, not his Top Gun salespeople. Our Infantry owner needed to learn to manage confrontation and conflict as the natural course in leading Top Guns.

By helping him stick to his guns, we were all rewarded to see this financial agency eventually swell to twice the size of his original organization. Our Infantry owner's company became a mecca for salespeople seeking a fine opportunity. By then, he had learned to operate from sales goals that he could document. Once he had the confidence to

76

manage performance, not personalities, this Infantry owner stood a chance at winning his civil war.

However, he will have to fiercely defend against his natural peace-keeping management tendencies to survive. If he returns to being a compliant and accepting leader, our Infantry owner will be overrun once again by his Top Guns.

Rage: An Infantry Paradox

One of the secrets of being Infantry soldiers is their fear of anger and conflict. It is this extreme discomfort with confrontation that prompts Infantry soldiers to seek other means of surviving their civil war in the workplace. Among their avoidance techniques, one is to be overly friendly to everyone. Helpful, tolerant, patient listeners, and *durable*, Infantry soldiers work diligently at keeping their internal conflicts from exploding. It is hard saying "Yes" when you feel "No," but our Infantry soldiers do it all the time. And, the Top Guns and Palace Guards love it!

"But, just like the straw and the camel's back, eventually our Infantry come out fighting mad."

But, just like the straw and the camel's back, eventually our Infantry come out fighting mad. Loud, blaming, and hurt, Infantry soldiers cannot believe all their kindness shown to others went for naught. How could the world treat the Infantry so badly, when they in return had treated everyone so "nice"? It is this keen sense of betrayal that triggers the Infantry's rage. What the Infantry doesn't see is how their overreliance on keeping the peace creates raging emotions.

I have found the fiercest battles being waged in organizations where management's focus is on keeping employees happy. Internally focused organizations tend to miss external opportunities, engage in turf wars, with the resultant inflated cost of doing business and lost market share.

Fearful of hurting employees' feelings, one of our clients, a CEO of a large retail chain, could not stand to fire any manager. Instead, he horizontally moved poor producing managers aside, letting them keep their old titles and pay levels, then made room for their replacements. As a result, this CEO was paying over $600,000 in excess wages to employees who were not producing.

What prompted the CEO to seek our help? Angry and feeling betrayed, the CEO wanted us to help him not be angry. His remorse was acute. He was very unhappy at himself for losing his temper with his employees. However, what he needed help with was not how to decrease his anger, but what to do about his fear of terminating poor producing managers. Once he realized how expensive his fear was to his organization, this CEO terminated his nonproducing employees and erased the $600,000 wasted labor cost from his bottom line. And, his anger began to subside.

Coaches and Mentors

Infantry soldiers genuinely like people. We have found them successfully serving customers in many industries across North America. The Infantry seek careers as educators, administrators, medical professionals, accomplished musicians, and athletes. It is their patience and diligence to learn complex skills which makes them knowledgeable and agile experts. As leaders, the Infantry's strength is in developing others to become contributors to their companies. I believe the world of commerce cannot survive without the Infantry.

"As leaders, the Infantry's strength is in developing others to become contributors to their companies."

79

CHAPTER SEVEN

THE MP'S CIVIL WAR

Dr. W. Edwards Deming, a statistician and the father of the Total Quality Movement (TQM), is by definition an MP. Through early analysis, Dr. Deming believed profits  could soar when organizations dedicated themselves to quality work output. Rebuffed in the late 1940s by an economically arrogant America, he was tapped by powerful Japanese industrialists to bring his philosophies to their growing commerce. Eager to prove his theories, Dr. Deming willingly crossed the Pacific to begin teaching the Japanese worker what has now become a highly accepted, worldwide business approach. In less than 50 years, the Japanese image of being a country that produced cheap, poor-quality products has been transformed. As the twentieth century winds down, the Japanese now set the standard for manufacturing excellence throughout the world.

MP's love quality. Slavishly working to produce error-free work is the trademark of these soldiers. Spending long careers in search of excellence and the avoidance of mistakes, the MP's are fanatics about accuracy. They find themselves in technological careers, in medicine, in demanding sciences and research, and in administration as well as the world of finance. These perfectionists *need* precision-type work and they love complex details. Accountants are excellent examples of the MP professional. Their critical eye, always in search of errors, serves their clients well.

The IRS has little to gain from auditing MP prepared tax statements. The MP loves doing it right, the first time. They take their rewards from seeing work completed without a smudge, without a typo, with *perfect* columns, and well-chosen words or precise figures.

"The world of the MP is also a world of rules, procedures, and protocol."

The world of the MP is also a world of rules, procedures, and protocol. MP's write the policies and police those who are to follow them. They sit in stern judgment of those who would break a rule or turn in imperfect work. Often believed heartless, MP's believe the world is made right when everyone lives by the MP's high standards.

Natural critics, the MP's are impossible to please. No "A" is good enough! "It should have been an A+" is often their reply. Perfectionistic, MP's naturally doubt what they do, say, and produce will ever pass muster. They *know* they could have done it better, if only they had more time, more money, more ideas, more equipment, more weapons. The bad news is the MP also believes you could always do it better, too!

Many of those individuals who find a career in law enforcement are MP's. You will spot them from among Top Guns who also like being the tough enforcer, by the MP's crisp military neatness and cleanliness. Wrinkle-free uniforms, tight hair styles, weapons worn properly, and shiny badges are the mark of the MP. Rigid and demanding, MP's put in long hours mastering their jobs, perfectly. The MP is a precision machine, bent on making the world a better place.

"The MP is a precision machine, bent on making the world a better place."

THE BATTLEFIELD:
The Entertainment World
THE COMBATANT:
Barbra Streisand

Barbra Streisand had her eye on becoming a professional singer at a very young age. With a single-mindedness of an MP, she drove herself to become one of the world's most recognized and skilled performers. As an actress and director, her drive to have every movie scene perfect is well documented. When she recorded songs, Barbra spent many hours to assure herself she had achieved her highest quality recording possible. Once completed, she would worry publically that the song's recording could have been better. At the outset of a new production, her sound crews,

"With a single-mindedness of an MP, she drove herself to become one of the world's most recognized and skilled performers."

her film and editing crews, the supporting actors and actresses knew of Barbra's perseverance toward perfect outcomes. No one expected to go home early when they worked on a Streisand production. After a performance hiatus of ten years, Barbra finally returned to the song stage. What kept her away? Her fear of failure.

The Angst of the MP

The MP's are relentless in their self-criticism. During our many hiring interview training classes conducted throughout North America, a hallmark of an MP applicant is, when asked, "For what have others criticized you?" The MP applicant goes blank. He or she stares at the interviewer and struggles to recall such an event. After a painful silence, she gasps, "I can't recall a time when I was criticized!"

Of course, the Top Guns sitting in the hiring interview training express their disbelief with an "Oh, right!" They can't conceive of anyone not being criticized, because as Top Guns they are criticized all the time.

Do MP applicants give us phony answers? Are they criticized, but try to hide it?

In our many years of experience, we have verified that most MP's are not criticized *to their faces*. Instead, managers and people, who work with MP's, report they soft-pedal their criticisms. What causes people to bite their tongues instead of criticizing an MP? The MP is devastated by ANY criticism.

MP leaders avoid criticism through sheer diligence. Working long hours, often involved in many operational details, MP leaders carefully build their companies.

THE BATTLEFIELD:
   Western Retail Center
THE COMBATANTS:
   MP Owner and Top Gun
   General Manager

A wildly successful retail center enjoyed a regional reputation built carefully by the MP owner over a 15-year time period. He was fastidious in his marketing, his merchandising, and how the store's operations were conducted. Perfectionistic, our MP owner was involved in every facet of his business. He feared fully delegating to his employees because he knew he could do any job in the store better than anyone else.

> *"MP owner was involved in every facet of his business . . . because he knew he could do any job in the store better than anyone else."*

When he contacted us, he was seeking a trusted firm who could help him plan strategically for his future. A true MP, this owner had become narrowly focused and submerged himself in the day-to-day tasks of running a growing retail center. He reported he feared he would somehow miss his business potential or make a wrong move, given his style of short-leash management.

Since his early beginnings with us, this MP's company growth has been phenomenal. Our MP increased his business by 500 percent during a time when making a profit in retail *anything* was a struggle.

With our MP's success came a growing staff. We advised him to find a strong, entrepreneurial general manager to help him maintain the company's growth. We helped him hire a Top Gun. She was tough, bottom-line oriented, with a strong background in management.

Our Top Gun general manager was smart. She engrossed herself in the company's systems, learned the market, and prepared aggressive store objectives and sales projection goals for all the sales staff. The Top Gun liked this company. Heck, she was no dummy! She knew a profitable company when she saw it.

Private Heroes

"Our MP was not the most sensitive individual."

Our MP was not the most sensitive individual. After his Top Gun general manager had worked for him over two years, he announced to her he'd scheduled them both to attend a strategic planning session being held at our corporate Dallas headquarters. On his appointed day, our MP arrived at our offices looking very worried. He'd seen his Top Gun in the hotel dining at breakfast, he reported, but she had ignored him. Thinking he'd been snubbed, he fantasied she was unhappy and she was going to quit.

Sorting through the pretravel details with him, the MP admitted he'd not discussed airline reservations with his Top Gun. He had not asked how she was getting to the airport (many miles away), and he'd not given her any itinerary of their two-day planning session with us.

The final straw was though they were on the same airplane going to Dallas, the MP did not attempt to locate his Top Gun. Nor did he make arrangements for them to travel together from the airport to the hotel.

And what had the Top Gun done? She'd taken care of herself. Fiercely independent, she had not allowed herself to ask the MP about the travel plans to Dallas. Top Guns are not good at asking for help. When the MP did not offer her any trip information, she got her ticket, and on the scheduled day drove herself to the airport to catch the plane. At this point, she never thought about looking for the MP owner on the airplane. Once in Dallas, she hailed a shuttle and went to her hotel.

"Top Guns are not good at asking for help."

87

Loners

"MP's fear any help they offer could be wrong."

Control-freaks, MP's and Top Guns are famous for being one-person shows. Top Guns fear asking for help and the MP's fear any help they offer could be wrong.

Without any contact from her MP owner, the Top Gun general manager assumed she was to get herself to Dallas. When the Top Gun did not ask him questions, the MP assumed his Top Gun wanted to take care of her own travel plans.

Neither the MP nor the Top Gun felt good about their trip to Dallas. The trip was boring because they did not have anyone to talk to. And, lonely. It had not occurred to either one of them to ask the simple, friendly question: "How are you getting to Dallas?"

Awesome Experts

"Expert MP's are awesome warriors."

The expert MP is a paradox. They can conduct business just as tough as can Top Guns. Expert MP's are awesome warriors due to their blunt, dictatorial, tough negotiator style. They set their sights high and refuse to accept defeat.

THE BATTLEFIELD:
   Presidential Election
   1992
THE COMBATANT:
   Ross Perot

Many of us recall the excite-
ment of the 1992 American presidential elections.
It was during this time that Ross Perot, an MP,
made a bold decision. Blaming both the Repub-
lican and the Democratic candidates for dodging
the national debt issue, Ross offered his candidacy to the American people to be "an alternative." The new, third-party candidate jolted the
stupefied electorate. In cutting, blunt sound bites,
Ross defined the complex differences between the
candidates while giving the voters detailed, statis-
tical "infomercials" of his views on the country's
national debt.

   In quick order, Ross had thousands of volunteers flocking to his campaign, which he personally financed. He embarked on a nationwide
tour, speaking before millions of voters about their
fiduciary responsibilities to the children of
America. No sugarcoating politician, Ross spat
it out like he saw it. And, we loved him. Or, we
hated him. But there were very few who asked,
"Ross, who?" Overnight Ross Perot became a
national celebrity.

"Overnight Ross Per-
ot became a national
celebrity."

89

Ross's television personality was as sterile as his messages. In no-nonsense and composed presentations, he prompted us to do the right thing. He drilled us with complex facts and statistics. He forced us to think. By the end of the election, he had successfully hammered through to 20 million voters who cast their ballots for the Perot candidacy.

Ross lost the race not because what he believed didn't square with the American people. Indeed, they were alarmed about the trillion dollars being spent on failed federal programs and unproductive educational systems.

Ross lost the election because he was seen as too demanding in his insistence the country live up to lofty world standards. Paradoxically, professional politicians worried aloud that Ross was both a "loose cannon" and "too rigid." Ross's MP leadership style was viewed by many 1992 voters as both uncontrollable and too controlling.

Final Word

"Our MP's are our judge and jury in their fight for excellence in the workplace."

Our MP's are our judge and jury in their fight for excellence in the workplace. They keep score of those who didn't follow procedures or those who made mistakes. Poor team players when grouped with rule-breaking Top Guns, long-winded Palace Guards, or sloppy Infantry soldiers, MP warriors complain bitterly. However, MP's hate con-

90

troversy. Therefore, they will choose to air their disdain of other team members only to a selected and trusted few.

Once made aware of their natural critical tendencies, MP's must work diligently to stop taking a judgmental approach with others. Unrestrained, the critical MP can demoralize an entire team, department, or organization.

To avoid demoralizing others, the MP warrior needs to see the world as naturally imperfect and learn to operate less critically in such a world. MP's can learn to see the world as "half full" rather than "half empty." It just takes MP's practice and an increased awareness in being less critical and unwilling to resort to blame as a defense against fear.

This approach to change I call learning to operate from one's ROLE SELF when the job demands it, rather than relying only on one's REAL SELF. In the following chapters, I will cover each Hero-style's REAL SELF VERSUS ROLE SELF, in terms of the types of adaptations each will have to make to bring meaningful peace to the workplace.

"Once made aware of their natural critical tendencies, MP's must work diligently to stop taking a judgmental approach with others."

"This approach to change I call learning to operate from one's ROLE SELF when the job demands it, rather than relying only on one's REAL SELF."

CHAPTER EIGHT

CONSCIOUS HEROES: GENUINE LEADERSHIP

People tend to behave as their Hero-styles indicate when working in their organizations.

For example, Top Guns tend to control others to make results happen. One-person shows, Top Guns take risks that the other three Hero-styles seek to avoid. Whether inside an or-

"For example, Top Guns tend to control others to make results happen."

ganization as an employee or at the top as the leader, Top Guns like being in charge. Willing to risk it all, many Top Guns become company founders. However, once an organization has matured, Top Guns have great difficulty in developing others to succeed them as second generation leaders.

Palace Guards rely on charm, excitement, and strong verbal skills to get what they want. Superb marketers, Palace Guards are known for their abilities to "break the ice" and  attract strong people to them or to their organizations. Highly visible, Palace Guard managers fear others will not like them if the Palace Guard is required to take a tough performance stand with an employee. Rather, Palace Guards prefer to "win" employees over and convince them to do their jobs just because Palace Guards are so likeable. As employees, Palace Guards love to work with bosses who are inspiring and motivating.

"Other people can count on the Infantry to follow through, to show up and do their jobs with little need for fanfare."

Infantry warriors are the durable people within organizations. Other people can count on the Infantry to follow  through, to show up and do their jobs with little need for fanfare. Dependable, Infantry soldiers are found in the trenches of the world of work and leadership.

Infantry leaders also seek to maintain the status quo at any cost and many organizations have paid a very high price for "doing business as usual." Unwilling to face risks that change brings, many Infantry leaders die a slow death of competitive obsolescence.

94

MP's are our quality-control warriors and leaders. They are diligent in making certain the job is done right, on time, and under budget. Perfectionistic, MP's worry about everything, including those who do not worry enough. MP soldiers fear failure like children fear dentists. Procrastination is their common defense. The MP would rather do *nothing* than risk doing the wrong thing. Children would rather ignore cavities than have the dentist fix them. As testament, generations of parents throughout North America have led their children kicking and screaming into the dentist's office. And, many MP employees and leaders are overwhelmed by the work that continues to await them "back at the office."

"MP's are our quality-control warriors and leaders."

Real Self Versus Role Self: The Peacemaker

The concept of Real Self versus Role Self can be complex. In today's society where being one's self is highly valued and supported by many, to be anything other than your genuine self may seem contrived or false. We all have witnessed a person "putting on airs" or "being a blowhard." This is not what I am referring to when I discuss the option of a person fulfilling a business role in over-

95

"Many times it is our
genuine self that can
contribute to a work-
related problem."

coming a business problem. Many times it is our genuine self that can contribute to a work-related problem. For example, recall many Top Guns' strong need to control their environment. This need for control is highly valued during the early founding years of any organization. Top Guns have their thumb on the pulse of their organizations to ensure their goals, as they see them, are achieved. As companies grow and Top Gun founders grow older, their controlling behaviors, once their strength, then become the founders' liability. Smooth transgenerational change in organizations, like exquisite weddings, only happen by design. Yet, how many companies have you read about, maybe yours included, where generation power struggles between owners drained precious resources away from the organization?

U-Haul, the internationally known truck and trailer rental company, is a case in point. The founder, a Top Gun, is in a death struggle with his children for the possession of the business. Little transgenerational attention was given to U-Haul's next generation leader. In fact, no individual among the family was identified or agreed upon as the most qualified new leader. This led to the founder's children squabbling amongst themselves for the top spot in the U-Haul organization. The founder never effectively planned for the day when he would not be the guiding force within his own company. He could not let go of his control. His genuine self, controlling, became his greatest liability. This owner, acting his Role Self and letting go of control long enough to develop the next leader, could have been the company's salvation.

The concept of playing a Role, of being something other than your Real Self, is a new concept in today's marketplace. What would cause people to attempt to act as someone different from their real selves? The need to play a Role would be directly related to the demands placed on individuals by their environment, business, civic groups, and families. Can you recall, either by experience or by story, an individual who naturally is a tough, impatient, demanding individual, but can become a maudlin, soft-hearted, baby-talking owner to his or her infant or pet? Recall the popular movie "Three Men and a Baby." All three men were naturally tough, demanding, independent, and *manly*. Yet, when left to raise a little girl less than a year old, they all became suckers to her slightest whimper. The audiences loved these new daddies. It became a very profitable movie for the producers, *because* we could all relate to these men who stumbled into being a family.

There is a strong need for genuine actions, either at work or at home. However, being genuine does not mean being yourself, at all times, with all your "warts." This could be you, being overbearingly you!

Which behaviors of these three men were their Real Self styles? Which behaviors were displays of their Role Self styles? Which set of behaviors were more genuine? The tough, indepen-

> "The concept of playing a Role, of being something other than your Real Self, is a new concept in today's marketplace."

97

dent manly men or the deeply caring, cuddly soft men who nurtured a baby?

Though vastly different, tough and soft, one set of behaviors was very appropriate for work and the other set of behaviors appropriate for caring for an infant. This movie, "Three Men and a Baby" provides us with an example of Real Self versus Role Self in action. The puzzle is which set of behaviors, tough independent men or soft, sensitive men, is more real? Some readers may answer "Both!" They may be right. What this movie offers the reader is an example of how varied our behaviors toward others can be, when we are invested in bringing peace to our world. We can alter our behavior, if it is important or we can achieve our goals because of our behavioral shift. That is the concept of being Real Self versus Role Self in action. You can remain genuine and flexible.

"That is the concept of being Real Self versus Role Self in action. You can remain genuine and flexible."

To play a Role, people must be highly motivated to change their natural behavior. This motivation can be derived from strong leadership, insisting that departments form effective work teams. Employees can be motivated to alter their Real Self behavioral styles if they learn that by doing so, they get more of what they want and less of that which they do not want!

When to Play Your Role Self

When do you switch from your Real Self to your Role Self? That answer depends upon how well your current job description matches your natural Hero-style. If your job is being the CEO and you describe yourself as a Top Gun, much of your natural Hero-style already matches a CEO job. However, when learning to hand over your position or company to the next generation, you will need to learn to act the Role of mentor and patient coach.

"When do you switch from your Real Self to your Role Self?"

When organizations are led by leaders or managers who react with little thought to the ramifications of their behavior on others, employees become quickly demotivated by seemingly insensitive management. Managers who are too blunt, blaming, or impatient with their employees can significantly lower staff morale. Infantry managers who are reluctant to confront poor performers demoralize those employees who are performing well above standard.

Having worked with thousands of leaders and managers for almost 20 years, I have found that the most effective executives, like great Hollywood performers, are those individuals who can "act the part" that their companies and their jobs need them to play.

"Having worked with thousands of leaders and managers for almost 20 years, I have found that the most effective executives, like great Hollywood performers, are those individuals who can 'act the part'."

99

Top Gun and Palace Guard Partner Roles

A highly successful client, a Midwest retail chain, owned by a husband and a wife team provides a good example of Role Self concepts. These two leaders relied upon one another's Hero-style as a way to overcome their own "personality deficits." He was a Top Gun who had become fossilized by his need to be overcontrolling, while she was a live wire Palace Guard who energized her husband and the entire organization.

The Top Gun husband depended upon his Palace Guard wife to provide him the energetic excitement at work, and she leaned on him as her steadying "rock." He was overly controlling of everything and everyone, including himself. She was emotionally mercurial when the Top Gun would not okay an advertising expense she believed was essential to attracting customers. Their revenue growth was good, but their staff's lack of excitement for serving their customers threatened the company's long-term profitability. While this couple enjoyed a mutually rewarding personal life, there were disquieting signs their natural Hero-styles were negatively affecting the company's bottom line.

100

During a series of Leadership Training seminars, our Top Gun husband and Palace Guard wife were given the opportunity to observe their natural Real Top Gun and Palace Guard selves. Our Top Gun realized his emotionally-closed style was browning-out his excitement for the business. Our Palace Guard realized she thrived on the excitement of quick changes which did not allow her to plan for the company's advertising campaigns.

In Leadership Training role-plays, our Top Gun was asked to act *as though he were excited*, while our Palace Guard was asked to *plan* for the company's advertising campaigns. The Top Gun was invited to "act as if" he was truly excited, while the Palace Guard was invited to "think" about developing a 12-month advertising calendar.

During their Leadership Training, the Top Gun and the Palace Guard were encouraged to "act their Roles" which their organization desperately needed of them, instead of naturally reacting as Top Guns or Palace Guards to many of their business circumstances.

"During their Leadership Training, the Top Gun and the Palace Guard were encouraged to act their Roles' which their organization desperately needed of them."

After completing the Top Gun and Palace Guard leadership Role Self training, the Top Gun recently showed up for a subsequent Leadership Training seminar in a brightly colored shirt. He led his group of fellow leaders in an exciting, energizing cheer! He further reported

"*The company is coming alive with the excitement of meeting and exceeding their customers' expectations.*"

he had conducted staff meetings just for the sole purpose of creating excitement among his employees for serving their customers. The company is coming alive with the excitement of meeting and exceeding their customers' expectations.

The Palace Guard wife is still highly energized, but she is also aware that her strong need for excitement and to feel liked by others are major liabilities to her company's bottom line.  She is now willing to think and make decisions that are good for her company rather than just seek the excitement gained from quick changes or acceptance from her employees.

Peace in the Workplace?

"*How can we bring peace to the workplace civil war? By learning to act the Role your jobs require of you.*"

How can we bring peace to the workplace civil war? By learning to act the Role your jobs require of you. If your job requires you to be patient and an attentive listener, but you tend to be impatient and a poor listener, then your Role will be that of a patient listener. This role-acting means you will have to learn new behaviors and practice them in order for these new Role behaviors to become second nature to you.

102

Just biting your tongue does not a patient listener make. Instead, learning to ask open-ended questions, such as "What could I do differently to make your job easier?" is an excellent method for impatient listeners to use to increase their listening attention span. Taking notes while the other person responds to your open-ended question further increases impatient listeners' capacity to pay attention.

Awareness, Desire, and Practice

Having read the book to this point suggests you already have gained awareness of what Hero-style best describes you. Knowing this about yourself is the beginning step to learning what Role Self changes, if any, you may have to make to meet your job requirements and reduce work conflicts. Learning about yourself can add excitement and a greater sense of your personal empowerment at work. As you decide what Role you will act to better meet your workplace challenges and reduce work conflicts, you are proactively bringing peace to your company or department. By knowing how to play your Role well, you can resolve your workplace disagreements or Hero-style conflicts.

"Having read the book to this point suggests you already have gained awareness of what Hero-style best describes you."

Awareness

Your Hero-style is a powerful shaper of your behavior. With little thought from you, your Hero-style approach can automatically kick-in allowing you to behave in a way that is familiar to you. However, when your familiar behavioral style interferes with your effectiveness as an employee or employer, this is when you can consider your Role Self approach. By selecting to act as your Role Self, this behavior may be better suited to your work situations or conflict resolutions.

By choosing to act rather than react to business situations, you will be more in control of yourself and your work environment. You will get more of what you want and less of what you do not want. You can be proactive in making things happen which can help you more effectively meet your business responsibilities. Learning to act rather than react is an important step toward reducing your workplace civil war.

Desire

In order for you to become skilled at playing the Role your job requires of you, you must *want* to be more effective or more successful at meeting your responsibilities. Without the desire to change your behavior, little change will occur.

Our driving force statement at TSI, "Practice the principle that all performance is based on belief" embodies the belief that individuals are at cause in their world. If you do not like what is happening to you at work, change it. It is only when you believe you are responsible for what happens to you that you will have taken a big step toward making your life work for you.

Practice

Your Hero-behavioral style described in this book defines both your work strengths and your work liabilities. Study the following chapters that correspond to your chosen Hero-style. Learn which of your Hero-style Real Self behaviors are helping you achieve what you want at work and in your world. Then pay particular attention to those Hero-style behaviors that are your workplace liabilities. It is here, among your liabilities, you may find clues for which Role you can choose to act out to reduce job conflicts or inefficiencies created by your Hero-style liabilities.

Changing natural behavior habits is challenging. New behavior, your Role Self, requires practice, awareness, and your commitment to change your Role Self behavior when it doesn't meet your work demands.

The following four chapters illustrate how you can alter your Real Self behaviors and become more artful in applying your Role Self behaviors. Those Role Self behaviors can reduce your civil war and may increase your job effectiveness.

CHAPTER NINE

THE TOP GUN ROLE SELF

- Top Gun Leader
- Top Gun Employee
- Top Gun Team Member

THE BATTLEFIELD:
Successful Retail
Operation
THE COMBATANTS:
Top Gun CEO and His
New Infantry Sales
Force

A high-profile retailer in the South called TSI asking our help in finding him Infantry warriors for his fast-paced sales floor. The Top Gun owner had made recent changes in his operation, one of them being to replace sales commissions with straight salaries. It was the Top Gun's belief the few Infantry salespeople already on his sales floor were taking better care of his retail customers than his Top Gun salespeople. With this insight, he decided to replace his Top Guns.

"With this insight, he decided to replace his Top Guns."

The Top Gun owner was also fed up with the challenges of managing other Top Guns in his organization. The historic makeup of his sales floor had been comprised almost totally of Top Guns. Fast-paced, commission-oriented, his Top Gun salespeople cruised the sales floor like fighter pilots. They were everywhere, hitting on anyone who stood still or appeared like sitting ducks waiting for the "kill." The Top Gun sales force was aggressive, bold, fast, eager to make a dollar off anybody.

"Top Guns challenge management as a fact of business. They love being in control."

Top Guns challenge management as a fact of business. They love being in control. They love making money. They love organizing others to produce and perform in their jobs. Top Guns love having the freedom to call the shots and can intimidate anyone who attempts to manage their performance. Fiercely independent, Top Guns hate answering to anyone, even another Top Gun.

"Fiercely independent, Top Guns hate answering to anyone, even another Top Gun."

Our Top Gun owner had it up to his eyeballs with his Top Gun salespeople. He wanted "can-do" salespeople who followed his orders, practiced his selling systems, and did what it took to make his customers happy. When the Top Gun owner said "Jump," he wanted his salespeople to say "Yes, Sir!" one hundred percent of the time. He wanted the Infantry.

The Role of a Top Gun

The changes this aggressive Top Gun entrepreneur made were enormous ones. He turned his organization upside-down in his strong belief that Infantry salespeople would better serve his customers and produce bigger sales. This Top Gun also believed by just hiring the right Hero, he would get the performance he wanted. Our Top Gun owner was in for a big surprise.

Infantry salespeople do, indeed, take "better care" of listening to their customers. Infantry salespeople have the patience to listen to customers who need help in thinking through their purchases.

> *"Infantry salespeople have the patience to listen to customers who need help in thinking through their purchases."*

In our extensive work with sales forces throughout North America, we have found Infantry salespeople often rely on their information-gathering processes and their product knowledge to be successful closers. Patience rather than aggressive closing techniques is the selling tool the Infantry salespeople use to win the trust of their customers.

To be successful, the Infantry streamline or follow systems. Once confident, they become wed through thick or thin to their systems. Our Top Gun owner did not fully appreciate this critical fact when seeking to convert his sales staff of Top Guns to the Infantry.

> *"To be successful, the Infantry streamline or follow systems. Once confident, they become wed through thick or thin to their systems."*

In the past, his Top Gun salespeople required little of him in the way of sales training. They

109

were naturally aggressive and bold enough to ask for the sale even when they did not have the confidence of their customers. The Top Guns' need for little sales training in sales techniques suited the Top Gun owner just fine. He had no patience to develop and follow through on a sales-training program.

When his organization was young, our Top Gun owner was happy that his Top Gun salespeople "took initiative" and didn't take "No" as an answer from their customers. The Top Guns didn't worry as much about dissatisfied customers back then as retailers do today. Heck, from the 1960s through the early 1980s nobody could fail at retailing. It was great! Customers bought even though abused or ignored by poorly-trained salespeople. And, it was the Top Gun salespeople's ability for risk-taking and their refusing to be turned aside by customer objections that originally built our Top Gun's business. He was thrilled with his Top Guns' performance as long as he looked at only his bottom-line volume.

It wasn't until later when our Top Gun owner wanted to institute more sophisticated systems throughout his stores that he met ongoing resistance from his Top Gun salespeople. Confronting, bold, and demanding, the Top Gun salespeople are a force to reckon with. Our Top Gun owner began to lose control of his organization, one complaining Top Gun salesperson at a time.

It was at this time that the Top Gun owner also noticed his Infantry salespeople. They were

> *"From the 1960s through the early 1980s nobody could fail at retailing. It was great! Customers bought even though abused or ignored by poorly-trained salespeople."*

the quiet ones, those who were less provoking, and were more willing to follow his systems. The Top Gun owner wondered what his organization would be like if he had more of these tolerant warriors as salespeople instead of his many Top Guns. That's when he called us.

The Top Gun Leader Role

It was very apparent this Top Gun entrepreneur was going to hire the Infantry whether he was prepared or not. To insulate the Infantry from the bullet-like sessions that our Top Gun called "sales training," we began to discuss what the Infantry needed from Top Gun managers.

"Our Top Gun's new Role as CEO is that of providing systems and a predictable work environment to his Infantry sales force."

Our Top Gun's new Role as CEO is that of providing systems and a predictable work environment to his Infantry sales force. The Top Gun owner had to be available to answer questions and provide ongoing training as his sales staff developed its selling maturity. No longer could the Top Gun conduct sales trainings that only focused on aggression-style selling. He now must provide product training, training on how to greet and gain customer rapport, and how to stay in charge of the customer's buying decisions. Infantry salespeople are not Top Guns. The Infantry won't risk aggressive selling approaches with their customers. If forced to be aggressive with customers, the Infantry would rather turn the customer over to a Top Gun.

To be effective, the Top Gun owner had to set up systems for training both his new and experienced Infantry sales force. He had to develop selling steps that included: approaching the customer, greeting the customer, overcoming customer objections, and asking the customer for the sale.

No longer could our Top Gun entrepreneur rely on his Top Gun sales staff's natural aggressiveness. Our Top Gun could no longer expect his salespeople to learn to sell successfully by watching other salespeople selling to their customers. The Top Gun had to provide his new Infantry salespeople with systematic steps to learn selling techniques. Without initial sales training and monitoring for ongoing use of his selling systems, our Top Gun would not create a successful sales force of Infantry salespeople.

The following are suggested Roles Top Gun leaders can consider in bringing peace and prosperity to their workplace:

REAL	versus	ROLE
One-person shows		Develop key employees and trust them
Impatient		Develop patience-building techniques
Intolerant		Recognize value of behavior diversity
Generalists		Develop systems from which employees can act and meet their goals
Poor listeners		Use open-ended questions, take notes, shut up
Overcontrolling		Delegate to trusted employees and inspect their performance

If you are a Top Gun, learning to act a Role to overcome your Hero-behavioral liabilities requires your commitment and willingness to practice new leadership behavior. Your skill at choosing to act rather than react to work situations will grow in direct proportion to your willingness to work at it.

Top Gun leaders' payoff in working more tolerantly with others can be very rewarding. No longer will civil war be waged at work. You choose your behavior. That is what empowerment is all about. When deciding to act, you no longer are easily drawn into battles or "get caught" in cross fires with those who report to you at work.

"Top Gun leaders' payoff in working more tolerantly with others can be very rewarding."

Motivating Top Gun Leaders

Top Guns leaders need the following:

- Freedom to act
- Independence from constraining policies or procedures
- Quick results
- Money as a reward
- Little routine detail
- No administrative duties
- Fast-acting employees
- Little distance between "cause and effect"

- Little routine follow-through
- No long-winded committee meetings
- Competent employees

Given these incentives, Top Gun leaders thrive in the business climate of risk and results. Without these essential motivators, Top Gun leaders become demanding and intolerant. These leaders have a short fuse for incompetent people or trivial interruptions and those who report to them better learn this quickly. If not, the hapless employee will wonder what "hit them" when his or her Top Gun leader fires them.

To Be More Effective

"Top Gun leaders need to practice tolerance and mentorship to develop their next level of leaders and managers."

Top Gun leaders need to practice tolerance and mentorship to develop their next level of leaders and managers. Without an early plan for succession, Top Guns find themselves turning their businesses over to individuals who lack the skill of leading the organization. National statistics seem to support an unhappy fact: Few first generation leaders prepare their second-tier leaders for effectively taking the reins of power. More than 80 percent of all second generation family-owned companies fail to survive.

Top Guns need to practice the following to be more effective:

- Spend time developing the next level leadership
- Increase listening skills
- Practice mentoring behavior rather than being a one-person show
- Share corporate information
- Bring others into strategic planning meetings
- Learn to delegate authority to trusted employees

Top Gun Employee

Nothing is so painful than to witness Top Gun employees struggle to work for someone else. Fiercely independent, Top Gun employees react with vengeance when employers curtail their freedom. The belief held by most Top Gun employees is that they could run the company better than the boss. Controlling, decisive, organizer of others, and results-oriented, Top Gun employees act as if they were the boss.

"The belief held by most Top Gun employees is that they could run the company better than the boss."

Top Gun Employee Roles

In a Midwest venture capital organization, a Top Gun receptionist had terrorized the entire staff, including the CEO, with her strong-handed control. No decision was made unless Susie agreed to it. She was an excellent receptionist and had become an essential person in completing the company's complex work output. She "helped" the CEO by organizing schedules, deciding priorities, and even influencing the CEO's decision-making process.

Everyone considered for employment at this company had to pass Susie's critical eye. Even worse, the CEO continuously worried that new employees wouldn't get along with Susie because of Susie's demanding nature. Susie had emotionally taken over the organization. She was its "informal leader." From the organizational chart perspective, Susie ruled the company from the lowest reporting line level.

"We helped the CEO establish performance objectives for Susie that were commensurate with the receptionist's job description."

Now, Susie would have to be *highly* motivated to want to change things at work. Why would she want anything to change? She had the best of all possible worlds, except enough money and a bigger job title. In our work with this organization, we helped the CEO establish performance objectives for Susie that were commensurate with the receptionist's job description. We also laid out performance objectives for the CEO and all other company positions. Once the job descriptions were in place, the CEO began to limit Susie's behavior if she strayed into other performance areas outside her own.

With corporate objectives defined and job descriptions in place, the CEO had a better grasp of the contributions he could expect from his employees. From a performance level, he began to develop Susie's natural leadership skills within her current title of receptionist.

"From a performance level, he began to develop Susie's natural leadership skills within her current title of receptionist."

The ball was now in Susie's court. She could run with it, but she must know she is running in her boss's court. Susie's greatest learning as an employee is how to work inside someone else's company. If Susie could learn this, she would be an enormous contributor to the company. Without adhering to management's guidance, Susie will continue to be the source of this organization's civil war.

The following suggestions are for a Top Gun employee to consider when selecting his or her work Role:

REAL	versus	ROLE
Independent		Follow guidelines and expectations set by boss
Generalist		Pay attention to job details and complete them as part of the job
Blunt communicator		Be aware of how strongly you come across to others
Decisive		Agree which decisions you can make before you make them
Challenge to manage		Decide to perform in someone else's company as employee

If you are a young Top Gun, this set of Roles may pose both a challenge and an opportunity for you. Owners and executives *need* Top Guns to groom as future leaders. What most executives shy away from when searching among the ranks for new blood are those Top Guns who have not learned how to operate in someone else's company. If you want to be on an exciting career track, learn to follow your boss's lead. Practice asking permission before forging ahead. Seek management input and work cooperatively with others. Consider the above steps as excellent shaping experiences for an up-and-coming company star. YOU!

Managing Top Gun Employees

"You, no doubt, have felt demoralized by working under management you did not respect. If you look carefully, you may also see that you demoralized others who worked alongside you."

If you are a Top Gun with years of experience working for others, you have had your share of learning challenges. You, better than most, know the Top Gun employee's struggle to work for someone else. You, no doubt, have felt demoralized by working under management you did not respect. If you look carefully, you may also see that you demoralized others who worked alongside you. Learning to communicate as part of a team, being tolerant of those employees who are not Top Guns, and learning to relate to the other Hero-styles can be your continuing professional challenge and opportunity.

To be more effective, Top Gun employees need the following:

- Defined job descriptions
- Clear understanding of their limits
- Solid job training
- Freedom to follow through on job demands
- Financial rewards
- Quick response to their ideas
- Little constraining details
- Short answers
- Understanding of the results gained from completing routine administrative work
- Delegation of workload when necessary (avoid one-person shows)
- Respectful management

If you are a Top Gun employee who works alongside others, you may find it beneficial reading the following suggestions for team players.

Top Gun Team Player Roles

When organizations attempt to control their labor costs and maximize employee productivity and customer satisfaction, executives often turn to work team formation. The self-directed team and the directed-team concepts have been on the American scene since the early 1960s. Managers have assigned employees to teams according to their past work projects or based their team assignments on the population of customers that employees historically served. However, little management attention has been given to team assignments based on the Hero-styles of team players until this book.

"No team member chafes more at working within a team than Top Guns."

No team member chafes more at working within a team than Top Guns. Top Guns are antithetical to team functioning. Top Guns would rather do it themselves than rely on any group for results.

Disliking committee meetings because of long-winded Palace Guards, wishy-washy Infantry, or nay-saying MP's, Top Guns quickly sabotage teams by either taking over team leadership or mentally checking out of boring team meetings.

"Top Guns are impatient, demanding, intimidating, poor listeners, and disrespectful of Hero-styles different from their own."

Nothing creates an ulcer faster in Top Guns than reaching decisions by committee. Top Guns are impatient, demanding, intimidating, poor listeners, and disrespectful of Hero-styles different from their own. However, having a team comprised solely of Top Guns is to guarantee a bloodletting struggle for "who's on first!"

For Top Gun team players to more fully contribute to their team goals, the following Role suggestions apply:

REAL   versus   **ROLE**

REAL	ROLE
One-person shows	Operate from team objectives
Result-oriented	Ensure team goals are well defined
Impatient	Set deadlines and work from agreed times and agendas
Poor listeners	Ask open-ended questions, take notes, shut up
Intimidating	Secure team role assignments and insist on maintaining them as assigned
Confrontive	Develop a plan for dealing with team conflict *before* the controversy occurs

The following graph indicates which Hero-styles the Top Gun team member naturally relates well to or finds difficult to work alongside.

Style Rapport	Team Member	Excellent		Good		Fair		Poor	
		1	2	3	4	5	6	7	8
Top Gun	Top Gun			✓					
Top Gun	Palace Guard							✓	
Top Gun	Infantry						✓		
Top Gun	MP							✓	

When a Top Gun team member works with a team that has well-defined team goals and timelines in which to meet them, Top Guns find themselves more team-oriented.

Style Rapport	Team Member	Excellent		Good		Fair		Poor	
		1	2	3	4	5	6	7	8
Top Gun	Top Gun	✓							
Top Gun	Palace Guard			✓					
Top Gun	Infantry		✓						
Top Gun	MP			✓					

Companies are not going to reject the concept of team formation as a cost-cutting and performance-enhancing model anytime soon. Therefore, for those Top Guns already functioning inside a team, by following the above suggestions you can begin to bring peace and prosperity to your workplace team.

Top Gun Team Summary

"As a Top Gun, insist on the team staying focused on their goals."

As a Top Gun, insist on the team staying focused on their goals. You can also insist the team stay focused on gaining results by setting project deadlines that are good for the organization's bottom line. Measure your results and report them to your team. By keeping your team results oriented, you will find your tolerance for your team increasing. Your team needs you, but you must learn to pull as a group of one. You have the Hero-style that can keep your team on target and accomplish established team goals. Without you, your team could drift into endless committee meetings and produce little meaningful results. You are a key player on your team, so play well!

CHAPTER TEN

THE PALACE GUARD ROLE SELF

· Palace Guard Leader
· Palace Guard Employee
· Palace Guard Team Member

THE BATTLEFIELD:
Banking Industry
THE COMBATANT:
Palace Guard President

A Midwestern banking executive sought our input regarding his leadership style as president of a corporate branch bank. His Hero-style was a Palace Guard. Our banking executive *looked wonderful* to others. He was the spark plug for all the banks' branch managers. Maintaining a high level of excitement and energy at the banks was this Palace Guard's personal goal. To that end, he made sure he was *always up* for his employees, even when he was personally feeling very down.

The enormous drain of energy he was experiencing from his self-imposed "spark plug goal" was causing him significant personal problems. He had no energy left for his family or for himself. Yet he believed himself to be a poor leader when he couldn't provide his high degree of "motivation" to the troops.

When I inquired about his low energy levels that showed on his Hero-style profile, the Palace Guard president glossed over this information. He didn't want to hear about any low energy levels, much less his own. He couldn't be down, not when his troops counted on him to be UP! It wasn't until I challenged him directly that this Palace Guard president admitted he was feeling "out-of-gas."

This admission made him fearful, because he knew he couldn't keep up the charade of being the bank's "Mr. Excitement." His fear was if he looked depressed or down, *everyone* at all the banks would emotionally collapse in a heap, like deflated balloons. He didn't question his fear or whether his expectation that everyone would collapse if he appeared down or tired was realistic. He just took on the assignment of being the company's cheerleader with the strong belief that if he didn't, something terrible would happen to his employees.

It was difficult for this Palace Guard president to step back and find alternatives to keeping his staff productive and excited, other than

"He believed himself to be a poor leader when he couldn't provide his high degree of 'motivation' to the troops."

"He didn't question his fear or whether his expectation that everyone would collapse if he appeared down or tired was realistic."

offering them a direct intravenous pipeline to his energy core. Many of his employees were Infantry and MP's. This Palace Guard executive did not know that to get them excited about serving customers meant providing them predictable and structured work environments. Since predictable and structured work environments bored the Palace Guard executive, he believed consistency and secure job benefits would bore everyone. It was very difficult for this Palace Guard to believe giving up his being a cheerleader and, instead, providing his employees with predictable work environments would result in better work performance and overall employee excitement.

"Since predictable and structured work environments bored the Palace Guard executive, he believed consistency and secure job benefits would bore everyone."

The Palace Guard Leader Role

The following are Role Self suggestions for a Palace Guard leader:

REAL versus	ROLE
Loses objectivity	Focus on employee performance rather than personality
Plays favorites	Treat all employees fairly
Believes in motivation	Provide employees incentives based on their Hero-styles
Loses track of time	Keep clock in full view and maintain time commitments
Talks rather than listens	Ask open-ended questions and take notes to keep self from interrupting

125

Motivating Palace Guard Leaders

Palace Guard leaders are exciting people to work for. With Palace Guard skill, these Heroes can talk a great story and create in others a desire to join a winning team. Palace Guards look like *successful* leaders and can instill initial confidence in employees as long as the Palace Guard *also* delivers on bottom-line promises.

To be excited, Palace Guard leaders need the following:

- Challenging opportunities
- Feeling appreciated
- Exciting business plans
- Aggressive marketing agendas
- Personal recognition from management
- Time with people
- Change and variety
- Supportive administrative employees
- Little or no boring routines
- To work for progressive companies

Unfortunately, the Palace Guard can embody the phenomena often called "the empty suit": Looks good on the outside, but does not have the internal knowledge or job skill to live up to others' expectations. As a result, empty-suit Palace Guards find themselves changing jobs frequently,

"The Palace Guard can embody the phenomena often called 'the empty suit'."

searching for fast tracks with quick advancement, having few boring responsibilities, and making big bucks.

To Be More Effective

When Palace Guard leaders buttress their excellent external appearances with solid business skills, are willing to follow organization leads, and learn to stay within the company's operating budget, they can be worth a million dollars to any organization.

To be more effective leaders, Palace Guards need the following:

"When Palace Guard leaders buttress their excellent external appearances... are willing to follow organization leads... they can be worth a million dollars to any organization."

- Objectivity in dealing with employees or work problems
- Well-defined job definition
- Expected results and aggressive deadlines
- Time management skill-building
- Increased listening skills
- Tolerance of others whose Hero-styles differ from the Palace Guard
- Adherence to agreed upon work budgets
- Prepare business plans before acting on them

"Palace Guards must accept the responsibility of leadership with a clear understanding of their tendencies for subjectivity and emotionalism."

Palace Guards are exciting leaders who can attract strong individuals to their work teams. However, Palace Guards must accept the responsibility of leadership with a clear understanding of their tendencies for subjectivity and emotionalism. Employees need their leaders to be objective and just.

Palace Guard Employee

Palace Guard employees enliven their offices and can be known by others as "can-do" people. Quick to respond to new challenges, Palace Guard employees love diversion as a way to avoid boredom. Palace Guards like to be active and enjoy a variety of work responsibilities that have them interacting with people.

These are the employees who can handle five ringing phones, four customers on hold, *and* eight people at their desk waiting for the Palace Guard's attention. Being sought after by people, feeling appreciated, and getting public acknowledgment of work achievements are what make Palace Guard employees chirp with job satisfaction.

"Palace Guards are in their element when they are in the people business."

Able to soothe the ruffled feathers of disgruntled customers, Palace Guards are in their element when they are in the people business. Palace Guards create upbeat work environments as long as the Palace Guard is getting his or her work needs met by management. Public recogni-

128

tion, variety, excitement, opportunity, people-interaction, and money—in that order—are powerful incentives to keep Palace Guards performing at their jobs.

However, when personally disgruntled, Palace Guards can become emotional and verbally attacking. Moody and prone to personalizing work issues are common liabilities of Palace Guards. Their work output can be erratic according to the mood they are currently experiencing. When Palace Guards are up, they are very, very UP! When Palace Guards are down, they are very, very DOWN! Unmanaged, Palace Guards are masters at beginning political wars in the workplace.

"When personally disgruntled, Palace Guards can become emotional and verbally attacking."

Palace Guard Employee Roles

The following are some Role suggestions for the Palace Guard employee:

REAL versus	ROLE
Subjectively reactive	Stay focused on performance issues: "What is the business problem?"
Talks rather than listens	Ask open-ended questions and take notes
Poor with time management	Set timelines for project completion, arrive early for appointments
People over paperwork	Complete all paperwork as assigned, accurately, and on time
Overspends budget	Stay within agreed upon budgetary guidelines

129

Paying attention to the daily functions, internal structures, and accepted protocols of organizations and departments can assist Palace Guard employees in becoming valued company resources.

Managing Palace Guard Employees

"Learning to focus on completing the mechanics of the job and following through on task assignments in a timely manner can increase the Palace Guards' value to management tenfold."

Learning to focus on completing the mechanics of the job and following through on task assignments in a timely manner can increase the Palace Guards' value to management tenfold. Add to this the Palace Guards' agreement to stay poised and professional rather than emotional and reactive, these Heroes could virtually write their own ticket on the career track of any organization.

To be more effective, Palace Guard employees need the following:

- Well-defined job descriptions
- Strong and objective management
- Increased listening skills
- Challenging task deadlines
- Time management
- Working within agreed upon budgets
- Pleasant working conditions
- Progressive management
- Variety and change

130

When managed by managers who understand the Palace Guards' penchant for drama and emotionalism, these employees can be highly productive. Without strong management, however, these same high producers can create enemies among the company's troops. Therefore, it is essential Palace Guards are guided by firm as well as understanding managers.

Palace Guard Team Player Roles

Palace Guards are natural team builders. Their basic tenet: "Any job worth doing by one person will be better done if there are at least two more!" Palace Guards love being with people. Having to spend time with others and getting to call it a "team meeting" can be heaven to Palace Guards. Team meetings provide the Palace Guard forums upon which to stage their ideas and win fellow teammates over to their side.

"Palace Guards are natural team builders."

Easy conversationalists who imagine themselves successful team players, Palace Guards quickly seek the limelight of team forums. They volunteer to be the "chairperson" or the "leader" when presenting the team's ideas to upper management. Palace Guards also present themselves as team "cheerleaders," to which their team gladly elects them.

Palace Guards love to lead and we love to let them. They make us look good, sound good, and feel good as long as we can listen to them. They need attentive, if not adoring, audiences. However, when challenged for the spotlight, Palace Guards' positive veneer begins to crack.

Palace Guards have difficulty listening to anyone other than themselves. Once team members ask for or demand spotlight equality in which to present their ideas, Palace Guards' "flags" fly a little lower. They are demotivated by loss of attention from their team members. Palace Guards have a hard time being the team's spectator. Instead, they want to *be* the team's event!

Suggestions for the Role Palace Guard team members could practice are as follows:

"Palace Guards have difficulty listening to anyone other than themselves."

REAL	versus	ROLE
Loves to dominate team conversation		Ask open-ended questions and take notes
Poor listeners		Listen 70 percent in team meetings
Poor time managers		Watch the clock; allow team members equal floor time
Personalizes team		Stay focused on team issues, goals, and avoid taking members personally

Poor listeners, Palace Guards need to learn the art of active-listening. If Palace Guards set a new goal of talking only 30 percent during their next team meeting and listening 70 percent of the remaining time, their teammates *will notice*. Palace Guards can continue to get the attention they crave, but in a more constructive, team-building manner.

Palace Guards love meeting in groups, as this affords them the opportunity to interact with other team members. The following graph indicates which Hero-styles the Palace Guard team member naturally relates well to or finds difficult to work alongside.

"If Palace Guards set a new goal of talking only 30 percent during their next team meeting and listening 70 percent of the remaining time, their teammates will notice."

Style Rapport		Excellent		Good		Fair		Poor	
	Team Member	1	2	3	4	5	6	7	8
Palace Guard	Top Gun					✓			
Palace Guard	Palace Guard			✓					
Palace Guard	Infantry				✓				
Palace Guard	MP					✓			

When Palace Guard team members are attentive to sharing the attentions of the group with other members and staying on-point with meeting team goals, they can increase their team participation effectiveness.

Style Rapport		Excellent		Good		Fair		Poor	
	Team Member	1	2	3	4	5	6	7	8
Palace Guard	Top Gun			✓					
Palace Guard	Palace Guard		✓						
Palace Guard	Infantry		✓						
Palace Guard	MP			✓					

Palace Guards must avoid their tendency to personalize work-related issues and work relationships. Palace Guards must think before they emotionally react to events or people. However, to be a team member, Palace Guards unfortunately believe in the buddy system: "Be my buddy and I will feel like a team member."

Buddy System Backfires

In a small company in the West, a Palace Guard team member had difficulty objectively joining in her team's projects. She often complained her team was unresponsive to her and that they left her out when planning key team events. Rather than discuss her perceptions with her team leader, she found herself avoiding her team members and their meetings.

When alerted to the problem, the Palace Guard's manager evaluated the situation through interviewing the team members. What the manager learned was that the Palace Guard had overstated the problem and had taken personally the team's attempts to work as a group. They had tried, according to the manager, to incorporate the Palace Guard, but were rebuffed when they would not allow her to dominate team meetings.

"The Palace Guard was asked to establish team-building behavior goals for herself and to set a schedule for practicing them before her next team meeting."

The Palace Guard was asked to establish team-building behavior goals for herself and to set a schedule for practicing them before her next team meeting. One of the behavior goals the Palace Guard set was to listen 70 percent of her team meeting time. When she did speak, she planned to ask open-ended questions of her teammates and then write down their responses.

After her next team meeting, the Palace Guard's teammates reported how helpful her "great questions" were to the team's problem-solving processes. They were thrilled to have her on their team. This is what the Palace Guard was waiting to hear. Her relief at being welcomed by her team was palpable.

Palace Guard Team Summary

Palace Guards are extraordinary employees who can contribute mightily to their organizations. Their personable style allows them to meet and greet their public, customers, and fellow employees alike in a warm and exciting way. Palace Guards help us to feel welcome. They can make others believe they are the most important person in the room or in the world!

Marketing conscious, Palace Guards know how to promote themselves, their team, their product, or their company advantageously. Skilled communicators, they gain initial rapport with many audiences. Their ability to present ideas to their listeners in an intriguing and entertaining way makes our Palace Guards very valuable in getting team ideas in front of the decision-makers.

"Their ability to present ideas to their listeners in an intriguing and entertaining way makes our Palace Guards very valuable in getting team ideas in front of the decision-makers."

We cannot do without our Palace Guards. Once they learn to listen to others, to share fairly the limelight with their fellow team members, they can be both valuable contributors to team successes and be the impetus for getting projects, products, or services sold to the "universal" customer.

CHAPTER ELEVEN

THE INFANTRY ROLE SELF

- · Infantry Leader
- · Infantry Employee
- · Infantry Team Member

The corporate world is filled with Infantry leaders, who through their diligence, hard work, knowledge, expertise, or at the urging of family members, have taken the reins as  president of their organizations. These leaders differentiate themselves from Top Gun leaders by their reluctance to strive for their presidential Roles. Infantry Heroes are not natural leaders, but earn their positions as corporate decision-makers through their extensive expertise or company and family loyalty.

These Heroes are the employees who start at the bottom of an organization and work their way to the top or become the company expert in their field. Technical, diligent, patient, and thor-

"Technical, diligent, patient, and thorough learners, it is our Infantry warriors who seek to be indispensable to their organizations."

ough learners, it is our Infantry warriors who seek to be indispensable to their organizations. Through this effort, the Infantry believe they and their organizations will survive.

THE BATTLEFIELD:
   Western Distribution Center
THE COMBATANTS:
   Infantry Director of Sales and Palace Guard Owner

In a distribution center in the West for a major floor covering manufacturer, a young college graduate was hired as a territory "sales rep." Twenty years later this sales rep became the distribution company's director of sales. He is an Infantry leader who through his diligence and expertise worked his way up the corporate ladder. However, once named the company's director of sales, this Infantry warrior faced a formidable challenge: a bored, young Palace Guard president, the third generation son of the owner. This Palace Guard loved having the title of "president," but did very little that was presidential for the company.

Because of the Palace Guard's neglect, no new technology or modernization was introduced into the organization to expedite greater expansion in distribution of its major manufacturer's products. Despite repeated warnings from the manufacturer, the Palace Guard president continued to spend more time out on the golf course than behind his desk. He couldn't conceive his company not having this national account. This manufacturer had been their major account for over 60 years! Besides, it was much more interesting to be out of the office. Off he went, day after day, to the golf course.

He *looked wonderful* out on the golf course, dressed in the latest golfing fashions, using state-of-the-art equipment to perfect his game of golf. It was hard for this Palace Guard to turn his back on this scene of success and face the stark reality of his situation back at the office.

However, reality struck. The major manufacturer withdrew the line, breaking a history of over 60 years with the distributor. Overnight, the Palace Guard's distribution company lost 70 percent of its business. And, where was the Infantry director of sales?

He was in the trenches being indispensable to the manufacturer by working with his sales force and increasing their market penetration. Knowledgeable, yet avoiding controversy, the Infantry director of sales was unwilling to press the modernization issues with an absentee Palace Guard president. The director of sales just worked harder at becoming the industry expert, hoping his sales force's dominance of their market area would be enough to forestall the major manufacturer from axing the distribution company. It wasn't.

"Knowledgeable, yet avoiding controversy, the Infantry director of sales was unwilling to press the modernization issues with an absentee Palace Guard president. "

The director of sales met with us in Dallas to discuss the twist to his career. This Infantry leader believed his career was dead, just like the Palace Guard's distribution company. The Infantry leader saw no options from which to build his future. He could only see the wreckage of the distribution company as his own.

Yes, he did little to force the survival issues with the Palace Guard president. He couldn't force the president to stay at his desk. Yes, he didn't confront the family to make them face their crisis. Yet, he couldn't force the family to invest in modernizing the company to meet the challenges of the twenty-first century. All that was true. Instead, the Infantry director of sales hoped that becoming the leading distributor of the manufacturer's line, they deserved the manufacturer's loyalty. Didn't they? NOT.

This Infantry leader is today still working within the floor covering industry. He is the director of sales for another organization, this one headed by a first generation, Top Gun. Combining the expertise of the Infantry director of sales with the vision of the Top Gun CEO promises to produce a powerful dynasty within the floor covering wholesale industry. In retrospect, the Infantry director of sales did not realize his "star" was attached to *his knowledge and his market identity*, not to the former distribution company. With the Infantry director of sales and his sales force went the former distribution company customers.

> "In retrospect, the Infantry director of sales did not realize his `star' was attached to his knowledge and his market identity."

To become more effective, this Infantry leader needed to face controversy that naturally accompanies the position of director of sales. Rather than avoid conflict, Infantry leaders must welcome differences of opinion as long as it is good for the business. By striving to make everyone "happy," Infantry leaders prevent the exchange of information that can provide valuable direction for the organization's future.

> *"Rather than avoid conflict, Infantry leaders must welcome differences of opinion as long as it is good for the business."*

The Infantry Leader Role

The following are suggested Roles Infantry leaders need to consider "playing" to be more effective for their organizations:

REAL	versus	ROLE
Peacekeepers		Stay focused on results
Avoid conflict		Be objective; confront issues with information not emotions
Hesitant managers		Manage performance numbers rather than personalities
Resist change		Realize change is a necessary part of doing business
Reserved communicator		Learn to exhibit excitement as integral to leader's job
Prefer listening		Set agendas, stay in control of groups and within meetings

Infantry leaders must stay focused on what the company or department has to achieve. Results are what today's economy demands of any

"Results are what to-day's economy demands of any business, just to stay in business."

business, just to stay in business. Many Infantry leaders would vehemently deny that results are secondary to keeping the peace. Yet, when faced with an angry and exploitive manager or employee, the Infantry leader's first inclination is to calm them down. (A Top Gun leader would "throw the bum out!") Infantry leaders just hope the "bums" will just leave on their own.

To avoid concession traps, Infantry leaders must set measurable objectives to manage employees. Without concrete data or performance numbers to shoot at, Infantry leaders are forced into dealing with the field's wide range of personalities. Emotionalism puts Infantry leaders at a leadership disadvantage. They are no good at staying in charge of highly emotional or demanding employees. To attempt to manage from this emotional position is akin to Infantry leaders operating from a one-down stance.

"Emotionalism puts Infantry leaders at a leadership disadvantage. They are no good at staying in charge of highly emotional or demanding employees."

Instead, hard and fast performance data is easier for Infantry leaders to manage rather than cope with an emotional employee's behavior. Either employees have or have not met their job objectives. Once Infantry leaders set up their organizations or departments as profit centers, they have a better chance of staying in charge and leading their employees.

Motivating Infantry Leaders

Infantry leaders lead from their knowledge. When leadership demands take Infantry leaders into civil war, they become their own greatest liability. These leaders are peacekeepers. But like the nuclear bomb with the same name, Peacekeeper, Infantry leaders have explosive outbursts if provoked long enough by the "enemy."

To experience greater leadership excitement, Infantry leaders need:

"When leadership demands take Infantry leaders into civil war, they become their own greatest liability."

- Predictable work environments
- Objective employees
- Harmonious and cooperative staff
- Well-planned change
- Work from well-developed management systems
- Time to think through strategic plans
- Knowledgeable employees
- Complex, well-established routines
- Recognition for a job well done

To Be More Effective

Employees need to know their managers or leaders are in charge. Therefore, Infantry leaders need to bring their product, industry, or techno-

"Employees need to know their managers or leaders are in charge."

143

logical expertise and their willingness and courage to assert their leadership with their staffs.

To be more effective, Infantry leaders need to:

- Keep their eye on bottom-line results
- Manage performances rather than personalities
- Create long-range corporate strategic goals
- Manage from numbers and concrete data
- Stay in charge of employee meetings
- Ask closed-ended questions more often
- Confront poor performance in timely manner
- Risk holding employees accountable to results
- Recognize tolerance can be over done
- Act on needed change
- Recognize leadership is controversial

Infantry Employee

"Infantry employees predominate in the workplace."

Infantry employees predominate in the workplace. Comfortable with demanding and complex routine, it is Infantry warriors who gravitate to jobs requiring patience, interest in repetitive tasks, mentoring, and customer service. The Infantry are the "glue" that holds businesses together, and they are loyal to strong leaders. They are known for their follow-through and diligence for task completion. It is no wonder Infantry employees are so much in demand.

THE BATTLEFIELD:
  Fast-Food Restaurant
THE COMBATANTS:
  Palace Guard Executive
  and Infantry Crew
  Members

Known for their ability to please customers every time, this fast-food chain prides itself on the quality performance delivered regularly by their employee crews. Infantry-like, systematic, thorough, interested in serving every customer patiently, the Infantry crew members epitomize the very best this company has to offer their restaurant customers. Regular operation training that is well attended and conducted in each restaurant ensures exceptional Infantry performance.

"Infantry-like, systematic, thorough, interested in serving every customer patiently, the Infantry crew members epitomize the very best this company has to offer."

The Infantry crews were comfortable with what the company expected of them because they were so well trained. Day after day, the Infantry lined up to prepare and serve the foods the company is famous for. Eager to please management, the crews were diligent in wanting to live up to company expectations.

Because the newest regional director, a Palace Guard, found her crews always so willing to follow corporate directives, this Palace Guard leader decided to informally ask her crews to survey their restaurant customers about their response to the newest food item on the menu. This new corporate manager had not worked her way up the corporate ladder by working in company-run restaurants. Instead, she had been hired from outside the company directly into a corporate management position.

What made this Palace Guard's request different from all other company directives was her failure to follow through with the related training. Her request was not followed by a formal survey-gathering training program. However, the Palace Guard believed this training oversight would not be a problem. She just wanted her crews to "talk with their customers."

"Without survey-interviewing training, the Infantry crew members would not have a systematic approach nor confidence to move out from behind their food counters to meet and survey their customers."

She was sadly mistaken. Without survey-interviewing training, the Infantry crew members would not have a systematic approach nor confidence to move out from behind their food counters to meet and survey their customers.

When the Palace Guard director visited one of the company's stores and learned no restaurant crew member had completed any customer surveys, she was chagrined. Angry and incredulous, she blamed the crew's lack of follow-through on their "laziness."

When she relayed this story to me, I suggested that rather than the problem being their "laziness," that the real problem was the Infantry's need for practiced systems, especially when faced with a new challenge.

Before her crews could comfortably go out from behind their serving counters, they needed role-play training and an interview script from which to survey customers. The Infantry *hate* sudden changes in their job assignments and especially changes in which they are expected to "wing-it."

Specialists, the Infantry have carefully mastered their tasks and gained skills for meeting their specific responsibilities. Like fine athletes who have perfected their sport, Infantry employees rely on their gained skills to exceed company expectations.

The Palace Guard could not believe what I was saying. She viewed the crew's survey-taking assignment as "simple" and "easy." FOR HER! She is a Palace Guard. She can talk to anyone, even strangers, with ease. It was because this executive did not fully appreciate the Infantry employees' need for training that her "survey the customer" project failed.

Infantry Employee Roles

Most Infantry employees become comfortable in their expertise and routines. They strive to find that employment comfort as a sign of career security. Once a job has been mastered, Infantry employees resist any change as a threat to their job confidence. Because Infantry employees generally resist change, their managers often view their Infantry employees as obstacles to progress.

What Infantry employees must learn to survive in the twenty-first century workplace is the capacity to flex with job changes as they occur. Job assignment changes will be commonplace in the next century. Those who cannot adapt will find themselves underemployed or worse, unemployed.

The following are some Role suggestions for Infantry employees:

REAL	versus	ROLE
Views change as bad		Accept change as necessary
Natural skeptics		Keep an open mind
Laid-back		Speak up and voice opinion
Stubborn		Ask questions, get answers
Black/white thinkers		Look for the "gray"
Wed to tradition		Find ways to innovate
Feels victimized		Take responsibility for own action

"Infantry employees will have to accept the concept of regular organizational change as healthy."

For Infantry employees to contribute fully to their organizations, they will have to accept the concept of regular organizational change as healthy. Companies that do not respond to external competitive challenges by changing their corporate directives will not survive. It is essential their Infantry employees understand their Role is to do what it takes to help their companies thrive, not just survive the next decade.

Managing Infantry Employees

Infantry employees look for strong management to be in control of their workplace. The Infantry rely on their managers to lead them, assign their work, and set responsibility priorities. Managers of the Infantry are also expected, by these employees, to take the business risks that they, the Infantry, would be loathe taking. Infantry employees seek environments in which they experience security and predictability. Managers who provide Infantry employees these important job features, earn their respect and management loyalty.

Keep in mind the following, if you recognize Infantry employees are already reporting to you:

- Provide fair business practices
- Provide security
- Be predictable
- Introduce change carefully
- Give Infantry employees time to adjust to change
- Provide them regular performance feedback
- Keep them focused on their results
- Let them own their responsibilities
- Recognize their tendency to "play victim"

"Infantry employees seek environments in which they experience security and predictability."

· Hold them responsible to their performance objectives

Soldiers require respectful, strong, and disciplined leadership. Under respected management, Infantry employees not only perform more effectively, they thrive.

Infantry Team Civil Wars

Infantry employees make natural team members. Cooperation, reaching a consensus, and listening to others are marks of Infantry team players. Interested in what others have to contribute, Infantry team members, like good politicians, enjoy spreading the responsibility for results around to others. The threat of risk is reduced and everyone is happy. Right?

THE BATTLEFIELD:
 *Upscale Cabinetmaking
 Firm*
THE COMBATANTS:
 Three Infantry Owners

In the Northeast, a company evolved through the efforts of a pair of brothers who were expert wood craftsman and one of their wives who ran the office. Expert, thorough, and

150

diligent, these three team players chose interlocking Roles to play to meet the challenges facing their growing enterprise. Scrupulously avoiding any hint of controversy, the wife dutifully served as the company's office manager and bookkeeper. All financial decisions were "agreed upon" by all three partners, though the wife privately held differing ideas about how to maximize their investments.

"All financial decisions were "agreed upon" by all three partners."

The two brothers were highly conservative when ordering materials and merchandise for the company. Instead of ordering in large truckloads, thereby saving money, the brothers chose to order supplies piecemeal. This piecemeal approach incurred smaller monthly bills, but the company paid higher prices for its materials. Though the wife disagreed with her family's method of ordering supplies and merchandise, she said nothing. She did not want the conflict with her family that her opinion was sure to create.

After much private soul searching, however, the wife decided to set aside company monies that remained after paying all the monthly business bills to go toward a truckload order. Rather than create a conflict, the wife-bookkeeper privately saved her growing "nest egg" for six months until she had enough set aside to order and *pay for* a full truckload of materials and merchandise.

It wasn't until after she *ordered the truckload* that the wife went to her husband and brother-in-law with the question: "Don't you think it would be more economical if we ordered our supplies and merchandise by the truckload, rather than piece-meal?" As she expected, both men vehemently disagreed. They said ordering a truckload on a monthly basis was too expensive.

Since the truck was on its way, the wife had to finally confess that she'd ordered a truckload and it was arriving in 24 hours. Her past six months of anxiety as she anticipated her husband and brother-in-law's negative reaction was well founded. They became highly frightened. It wasn't until she informed them the truckload was also fully paid for by monies she had saved over many months that the brothers finally realized their fear was for naught.

Rather than force the issue as a partner with her husband and brother-in-law, the wife had en-dured months of anxiety in private, rather than risk creating controversy.

Infantry Team Player Roles

"It is through this man-ner that the Infantry suffer needlessly. Their strong belief is that controversy is bad for businesses or partnerships."

It is through this manner that the Infantry suffer needlessly. Their strong belief is that controversy is *bad* for businesses or partnerships. However, in order for Infantry team players to fully contribute to their teams, they must be willing to act even when it will cause disagreement.

152

Roles that Infantry team members could play to decrease their personal team behavior liabilities and increase their effectiveness as team players are as follows:

REAL	versus	ROLE

REAL	ROLE
Peacekeepers	Recognize some controversy is healthy for business
Tolerant	Be willing to disagree if business requires it
Listeners	Risk stating opinions and listen to others' opinions
Resist change	Recognize change in business is inevitable
Skeptical	Look at both reasons why an idea or change can work and why it cannot work
Stubborn	Ask questions and view issues from a business need
Uncomfortable with new	Accept discomfort as a signal for open-mindedness not automatic resistance
Need time	Be willing to ask for time to read ideas or consider project materials

The Infantry are team workhorses. They believe in group efforts and are willing to follow through with the team's administrative demands as long as team members play fair. The following graph indicates which Hero-styles the Infantry team member naturally relates well to or finds difficult to work alongside.

Style Rapport		Excellent		Good		Fair		Poor	
	Team Member	1	2	3	4	5	6	7	8
Infantry	Top Gun					✓			
Infantry	Palace Guard			✓					
Infantry	Infantry			✓					
Infantry	MP					✓			

Naturally patient, Infantry team members strive to maintain the group's positive interactions by being cooperative and helpful. Team results must be well defined in order for the Infantry team members to stay focused on team goals. With agreed upon agendas and goals, the Infantry team members' capacity to work alongside other Herostyles for team results improves.

Style Rapport		Excellent		Good		Fair		Poor	
Team Member		1	2	3	4	5	6	7	8
Infantry	Top Gun		✓						
Infantry	Palace Guard		✓						
Infantry	Infantry		✓						
Infantry	MP			✓					

Infantry Team Summary

"*Infantry team members work cooperatively to meet everyone's expectations.*"

Considerate of their team members' schedules and deadlines of team projects, Infantry team members work cooperatively to meet everyone's expectations. Unless treated unfairly, Infantry team members will tend to volunteer for team duties before other team members. Treated unfairly, the Infantry can become roadblocks and stubbornly underserve the other team members. Thus, to avoid Infantry burnout and negative reaction to unfair team practices, Infantry team members need to ask that other team members share the team's workload.

CHAPTER TWELVE

THE MP ROLE SELF

- · MP Leader
- · MP Employee
- · MP Team Member

THE BATTLEFIELD:
Petroleum Service
Company
THE COMBATANTS:
MP Supervisor of Field
Operations and MP
Human Resource
Director

A major petroleum exploration and service company executive contacted us to help the company lower its cost of doing business by increasing the success rate of retaining field operators. By lowering field operator turnover rate by a mere ten percent, this Fortune 500 company stood to enjoy a significant gain in its competitive market share. At the time of the initial contact, however, the company suffered from over 100 percent turnover among its field operators.

Field operators are one of the lowest positions on the company's pay scale, but one of the most demanding in terms of physical labor, challenging working conditions, and family isolation. Oil field explorations occur in very isolated geographic regions, thus subjecting field personnel to extreme weather conditions and long periods of separation from their families. It is no wonder this position has such a high "mortality rate" among today's young men who are more use to air conditioning and Nintendo computer video games.

In the past, when oil exploration work had the allure of John Wayne and Hollywood, this company had little difficulty staffing its field operations. Many young men lined up to go out and "become oilmen" in the best meaning of the term. Field work was akin to young men experiencing their "Rites of Passage," becoming transformed as inexperienced youths into hardened, seasoned men. This was the career path of choice for young men seeking careers in the oil industry. However, with the glut in world oil supplies, the American oil industry fell on hard times. Ready applicants for field operations work also dried up.

The supervisor of field operations, an MP, was assigned by a Top Gun vice president the challenge of finding a quick way of increasing successful hires and tenure of their field operation personnel. However, the Top Gun was also anxious to avoid involving the Human Resource Department, which was famous for making slow decisions.

The Top Gun's message to the supervisor: lower field operator turnover *fast.*

It was obvious the MP supervisor had a lot at stake, but had very little idea on how to begin. When he heard about TSI's reputation for increasing a company's hiring successes, he was like a battle-worn soldier who had just found an escape hatch. He immediately enrolled in our Hiring School, seeking our EEO-approved systems to increase *his* successful hires. By hiring more qualified field operations applicants, the supervisor reasoned rightly he would also significantly decrease their turnover.

He *loved it.* MP's love having a business track to follow, thus guaranteeing them expected quality outcomes. Our hiring system was the way for this MP to meet the challenge of finding qualified field operators who would stay on the job. In his mind he'd found a way to increase field operator tenure and increase the profitability of the company.

Enter the Human Resource Director

All along we advised the supervisor to inform the company's Human Resource Department (HRD) of what he was doing to meet the Top Gun's turnover challenge. Placing personnel staffing problems outside the HRD did not make sense to us, and we believed this oversight could threaten the supervisor's entire initiative.

When the vice president of human resource, an MP, learned of the supervisor's staffing efforts, she was incensed. In her MP mind, it was not right those personnel practices and projects were being conducted outside her department. Her sense of correctness was threatened. She demanded to be updated by the supervisor on his actions.

This was the beginning of the end for the supervisor's turnover project and his use of our hiring system. We knew that any action the supervisor had taken without the human resource director's blessings was doomed. And, we were right. The human resource MP shot down all of the supervisor's initiatives and began her own lengthy analysis of the field operator turnover problem. She also severed any contact with TSI.

Within months, we read in our local newspaper of this petroleum company's demise. It was taken over in a hostile bid by another competitor. No wonder the Top Gun and the supervisor had such an urgency to show an increase to their bottom line.

Where had the human resource MP been in allowing field operator turnover problems to go unaddressed? Like any nondirected MP executive, she had buried herself in departmental details and lost sight of the looming external threat.

"In her MP mind, it was not right those personnel practices and projects were being conducted outside her department. Her sense of correctness was threatened."

"Like any nondirected MP executive, she had buried herself in departmental details and lost sight of the looming external threat."

158

Shortsighted and unaware of how to run her department as a profit center, the human resource MP became an unwilling participant in the company's hostile takeover.

The MP Leader Role

MP leaders seek perfection from their leadership efforts. Detailed, precise, feeling overly responsible for everything, MP leaders often become quickly overwhelmed by their work demands. Lacking the natural ability to prioritize, MP's approach every request or question as the most important thing facing them that moment. All challenges loom big and all problems potentially catastrophic. MP's believe ignoring any demand is an invitation to disaster. Liking everything in its place and a place for everything, MP's expect their employees to live up to ideal standards.

The way MP's can overcome their perfectionistic liabilities and, therefore, maximize their strengths as quality leaders is to "play the Role" of the leader. Focus on realistic expectations as well as the larger organizational needs. Naturally finding comfort in day-to-day details, MP leaders are easily seduced back into micro management. They must force their focus onto the organization's horizons and recognize realism as a meaningful goal.

"Detailed, precise, feeling overly responsible for everything, MP leaders often become quickly overwhelmed by their work demands."

"They must force their focus onto the organization's horizons and recognize realism as a meaningful goal."

By relying on the following Role Self suggestions, MP leaders can function more effectively in their organizations:

REAL	versus	**ROLE**
Perfectionists		Set range of goals to include minimum and realistic expectations
Worriers		Know what is possible and stop negative self-talk
Poor prioritizers		Set project's importance based on objective
Blamers		Take responsibilities for own errors, increase tolerance for others who are learning on the job
Procrastinators		Set realistic deadlines and stick to them

"MP leaders want to do the right thing, every time."

MP leaders want to do the right thing, every time. Making excellent professionals in fields that demand high degrees of skill, such as sciences, arts, sports, music, finances, and administration, MP leaders are diligent in their efforts to fill their organizations' needs. Eager to exceed all expectations, MP leaders often are their own worst critics. Negative self-talk serves to undermine the confidence and self-esteem of many high-powered MP leaders.

Motivating MP Leaders

Becoming kinder, softer friends to themselves, learning to accept human rather than godlike levels of performance, and finding satisfaction in jobs which meet realistic expectations can all help MP leaders lower their internal stress levels. Without these steps, MP leaders often fall prey to stress-related injuries and illnesses.

MP leaders need the following motivators:

- Predictable work environments
- Quality-control procedures to ensure accuracy
- Time to consider change
- Security
- Structure and company policies
- Help in prioritizing what is important
- Realistic expectations from self and others
- Regular feedback
- Constructive criticism essential to professional growth

To Be More Effective

MP's fear criticism, any criticism. This means MP leaders must learn the art of accepting constructive criticism as well as giving it to others. Without constructive performance feedback, employees do not have a realistic guidepost of whether they are meeting organizational performance standards.

To be more effective, MP leaders need to:

"MP's fear criticism, any criticism."

- Set realistic performance objectives
- Set a range of performance goals to avoid striving for only a goal of perfection
- Avoid procrastination
- Check their work for realistic expectations
- Keep agreed upon time deadlines
- Learn the difference between constructive criticism and destructive criticism
- Accept change as necessary for corporate growth
- Develop strategic, long-range corporate plans

MP Employee

"Diligent, thorough, persistent, systematic, detailed, and eager to work with very few errors, MP employees are the rank and file of many company offices."

Many organizations seek to hire MP's as employees. Diligent, thorough, persistent, systematic, detailed, and eager to work with very few errors, MP employees are the rank and file of many company offices. Administration, routine quality-control work, daily details, repetitive tasks, customer service, and complex analysis are many areas in which MP employees excel. They are at home in companies that afford them structure, consistency, predictable work environments in which safety and security are commonplace.

These soldiers love to make a secure workplace for themselves away from home: their desk, their phone, their coffee cup, their computer, and their privacy are very valuable to MP's. MP's take time to set up their offices just so, due to their need for structure and workplace organization. Everything has a place and there is a place for every thing.

Creatures of habit, MP's are the people who arrive like clockwork every day and have their routines for getting ready to start their workday. If forced by business circumstances to change their early morning habits, MP employees can complain bitterly. Preciseness is next to godliness is the MP motto.

"Rules are mechanisms that 'level the playing field'."

MP employees love company policies, especially those written and distributed to every employee. Rules are mechanisms that "level the playing field" and help MP employees predict work situations and outcomes. When everyone knows the rules, then risks for error are reduced. MP's want everyone to do the right thing. That way the MP feels safe. When rules change or shifts in work procedures occur suddenly, the MP's civil war begins.

"MP's want everyone to do the right thing. That way the MP feels safe."

163

MP Employee's Civil War

THE BATTLEFIELD:
   *West Coast Retail
   Chain*
THE COMBATANT:
   MP Executive Secretary

One of our west coast clients called one morning crying in real pain: "She's destroyed our billing system." The "she" in this case was the president's former executive secretary, an MP. She had been employed by this firm for over ten years and served as a key confidant to the Top Gun president for many of those ten years. She believed herself to be his "right hand" and essential to the smooth functioning of the president's office.

After going through corporate restructuring, this secretary "lost" her exalted position as executive secretary to the president, becoming instead the company's accounting clerk. In typical MP style, the new accounting clerk did not openly complain, but instead "appeared" to put her head down and work diligently as the accounting clerk. What she really did was to nurse resentment until it had become as big as Vesuvius: "How dare they demote her! After all she'd done for the president. Didn't he care about her?"

As her resentment crystallized, so did her retaliation action plan. Over the next year she slowly sabotaged the company's billing system until the day

164

she quit, without notice. It was then that the business office manager took a closer look at the accounting ledgers and realized they made no sense. Searching in the departed accounting clerk's office, they found invoices and receipts hidden behind filing cabinets, under stacks of papers, in the back of drawers. *Anywhere but* where they should have been. The withheld invoices and receipts represented hundreds, if not thousands of company dollars.

The company had no idea who owed what and to whom. The MP accounting clerk had exacted her punishment on the company for being wrongly treated by the president to whom she'd devoted ten years of her professional life. She had earned the right, so she believed, to better treatment than to be unceremoniously named "accounting clerk." She visited the famous MP "I'll get you later" motto on both the company and the company's customers.

MP employees have a strong sense of right from wrong. Needing to have predictable work environments, MP's go to great lengths to insulate themselves from sudden changes, interruptions, shifts in company rules or policies. Believing rules are made for everyone, MP employees are comforted by conformity and routine. When workloads are well ordered, then MP's believe they can meet most work demands. It is when chaos threatens that MP employees become fearful, resistant, and angry. Rigid and inflexible, MP employees hold fast to rules and procedures, even when facing company presidents.

"Needing to have predictable work environments, MP's go to great lengths to insulate themselves from sudden changes, interruptions, shifts in company rules or policies."

I'd Rather Be Right Than Make You Happy

In a small company, the company's Top Gun president was called suddenly out of the office. On his way out the door, he passed the newest administrative support person, an MP, who was seated at the front desk. "Would you let the office manager know I will be out for about an hour?" asked the president of the new MP employee. "That's not in my job description," replied his newest employee. Her MP reply left the president speechless! He'd not realized the extent to which MP employees *need to be right.* This MP's job description did not say specifically: run messages for the president.

It is essential managers of MP employees understand their strong adherence to established rules and protocols. Well-defined job descriptions must also include any exceptions to the rule. Otherwise, set schedules, written company policies, and company routines become etched in stone for MP employees. Asked to violate company rules or policies is akin to MP employees experiencing physical pain.

Perfectionism as a Fault

"Rather than fear mediocrity, MP employees need to better understand when mediocre performance is all that is needed."

To be more effective, MP employees must see their world differently. Operating in the world of Top Guns, for example, MP employees have to lower their high standards for perfectionism. Rather than

166

fear mediocrity, MP employees must understand when mediocre performance is all that is needed. Instead of agonizing over sloppy internal memos, typos, or worrying about details that have low priority to their managers, MP employees can increase their effective use of time by focusing on what their Top Gun bosses see as important.

MP employees are internally driven by anxiety, worry, and urgency. MP employees always think of what could go wrong first, rather than what could go right. Often appearing impatient under pressure, what really is occurring is the MP's sense of growing panic. Unable to prioritize, MP employees see *everything* as very important. When faced with minor errors, many MP employees react like the "sky is falling."

MP employees' fear of failure is the result of early programming by their families. In the eyes of the MP child, the family's survival depends on the MP child being perfect. Yet, paradoxically, MP children often believe themselves to be failures.

Demotivated by criticism, MP employees fall apart when openly criticized by others. Trying not to upset MP employees, their bosses avoid harsh criticisms so as not to undo their MP. However, pussyfooting around MP employees only serves to intensify their fear. Given no real feedback, MP employees assume they have failed their companies in some, unexplained, or unseen way. This is an example of the twisted thinking of MP employees: If it can go wrong, *it will*.

"Demotivated by criticism, MP employees fall apart when openly criticized by others."

MP Employee Roles

To increase their effectiveness, the following are some Role Self suggestions for the MP employee:

REAL	versus	ROLE
Rigid adherence		Be aware of ways to cooperate to gain results to rules and procedures
Fearful of change		Ask for notice of change beforehand, get defined instructions if prior notice is impossible
Blaming		Stay focused on business solutions rather than assign blame
Perfectionistic		Follow expected guidelines as laid out by manager
Procrastinator		Get schedules and/or priorities, avoid tendency to triple check your work (a time waster)

MP employees are the backbone of American organizations. Without them, the daily administration, business analysis, and quality-control work of the country would suffer. However, they require special handling by their managers.

Managing MP Employees

MP employees base their commitment to management on whether the manager is consistent, predictable, and knowledgeable. The MP manager may consistently be a jerk and predictably a de-

manding prima donna; however, if the manager is
also highly knowledgeable, a *really important person*, MP employees will tolerate management's
tacky behavior. The MP may be a long-suffering
employee and believe himself indispensable to his
boss.

Managers must keep in mind that MP employees thrive on the following:

- Structure
- Predictability
- Consistent feedback
- Time to complete tasks
- Help prioritizing responsibilities
- Realistic goals
- Constructive criticism
- Security
- Time for family
- Time to adapt to change
- Well-ordered change
- Quality-control opportunities
- Well-documented rules/procedures
- Everyone follows the rules/procedures

MP employees will be hit hardest emotionally by the changes being wrought in businesses
today. The downsizing that companies continue
to implement, the ongoing company mergers, the
growing number of temporary employees who are
now hired to complete projects or are hired part-
time by the hour all pose threats to the MP's sense
of security. To the MP, change is destabilizing in

itself. That an entire nation of businesses is experiencing change only increases the MP's belief that the "new" world is a harrowing place in which to make a living. Any deviation from the expected, the proven, or the long-established protocols can cause MP employees to panic. Managers can prepare for this panicky MP response by creating well-ordered change in which MP's are invited to participate beforehand. Time to prepare allows MP employees to vent their concerns and then find ways to buy in to the needed company innovations.

MP Team Civil Wars

THE BATTLEFIELD:
  Fast-Food Corporate Headquarters
THE COMBATANTS:
  MIS Department MP Managers and MP Employees

Back in the 1980s, one of the country's largest fast-food chains made a courageous decision to reconfigure their organization's headquarters in an attempt to reduce their cost of doing business.

As part of that move, many layers of management were eliminated throughout all corporate departments. The company's one department most affected by this executive decision was the

MIS Department. Predictably, the MIS managers reacted negatively to the proposed change.

The MIS Department had several hundred employees and about a third of them were mid-level managers who had earned their titles through hard work and company tenure. Perfectionists, a full-scale MP resistance to the reconfiguration dominated the department. Known throughout the organization for their predictable thoroughness, detail-orientation, and tough adherence to company policies, the company's MIS managers now proved to be a negative force to be reckoned with. A mutiny threatened.

"Perfectionists, a full-scale MP resistance dominated the department."

The "generals" of the company called in the calvary. An outsider, a hotshot MIS director with over ten years of management experience in Fortune 500 companies was brought in to deal with the MIS uprising. The new director, also an MP, had a fancy degree to go along with her impressive work experience. This combination of accomplishments, coupled with the director's no-nonsense communication style would be enough, so hoped the generals, to quell the MIS manager rebellion.

It wasn't.

When this newest MIS director was introduced to her new department, her MP employees went on full alert. Grumbling, irritable, and uncooperative, the MIS Department became a hotbed of MP open rebellion. Anger, fear, and whispered exchanges between the veteran MP employees and managers became commonplace for the new director.

"Anger, fear, and whispered exchanges between the veteran MP employees and managers became commonplace for the new director."

Being a supportive team to the new MIS director was out of the question for these MP's. They had lost their hard-won positions and status due to the company's restructuring. Who could they blame? They chose the new, blameless MIS director, even though she'd been on the job less than a month.

Within a very short time, the MIS director privately conceded defeat. She armored herself behind her desk and office walls, communicated with her MP employees mostly in written memo form, and sought to avoid any face-to-face confrontation. The MIS director never gained a foothold in this territory. By the time I had met her, she wanted out. To her credit, however, she continued to work for meaningful reorganization, rather than wave a "white flag" of surrender. But, she was already looking a for new opportunity with another company that included less hand-to-hand combat that accompanies restructuring.

"The MIS director never gained a foothold in this territory."

What this MP director may have had the company address before she arrived, was to call for the establishment of internal teams among the veteran MIS employees. These teams could work directly with management in bringing the new department structure rationale and changes back to the rest of the department employees. Then, the new MIS director would have been able to work through these internal MIS teams, instituting change rather than spearhead the hated changes and eventually becoming a symbol of the department's destabilization.

172

MP Team Player Roles

MP's make exceptional team players when they
agree with the purpose and the team membership
makeup. MP team players are very demanding
of excellence, both in what the team is expected to
produce and who is included on the team. MP
team members require rules, regulations, time
schedules, agendas, clearly-defined needs for
change, well-defined team outcomes, and agreement that everyone on the team will "play" the
same as the MP.

*"MP team players are
very demanding of ex-
cellence."*

When any of the MP team needs are ne-
glected by non-MP team members, the MP team
members become highly fearful and blaming. To
be more effective team players, the MP's need to
be aware of their team Role Self:

REAL versus	ROLE
Rigid with unexpected change	Be flexible by asking definitive questions
Fearful of errors	Set expectations that include both minimum/ optimum performance standards
Skeptical planners	Establish well-defined guidelines for entire team
Perfectionistic	Set doable goals that all can meet
Poor delegators	Assign tasks and hold team accountable
Worriers	Stop mind-talk that destroys realism, ask yourself if worrying gets results

The following graph indicates which Hero-styles the MP team member naturally relates well to or finds difficult to work alongside.

Style Rapport		Excellent		Good		Fair		Poor	
	Team Member	1	2	3	4	5	6	7	8
MP	Top Gun					✓			
MP	Palace Guard						✓		
MP	Infantry				✓				
MP	MP		✓						

When policies and team rules are well defined, MP team members are more effective in working for team results.

Style Rapport		Excellent		Good		Fair		Poor	
	Team Member	1	2	3	4	5	6	7	8
MP	Top Gun	✓							
MP	Palace Guard			✓					
MP	Infantry	✓							
MP	MP	✓							

"MP team members' contribution, at their best, is to the quality output of their team efforts."

MP team members' contribution, at their best, is to the quality output of their team efforts. At their worst, MP team members can be roadblocks to all team functioning. Too caught up in being right, fearing errors, and frozen in unthinking righteous rigidity, MP team members can shy away from fully cooperating with team formation and team efforts. Therefore, it is essential to capture MP cooperation from the onset of any team formation efforts.

MP Team Summary

MP team players require well-defined team formation plans. Worriers when there are too few guidelines, MP team players, more than the other three Heroes, need reassurance that the team's efforts will be judicious, fair, safe, and perfect. Since perfectionism is an MP liability, the MP team members need to learn to accept reasonable team output standards. Unless well-defined team performance standards are accepted by the MP, any efforts made by the team that does not measure up to the MP's sense of excellence are doomed.

"MP team players . . . need reassurance that the team's efforts will be judicious, fair, safe, and perfect."

CHAPTER THIRTEEN

A TREATY: QUELL THE CIVIL WAR

The civil war occurring in the American workplace is costing organizations hundreds of millions of dollars in lost productivity and lowered worker morale. Despite organizations making major investments in business training and trying to improve employee relations, most offices in America still experience intrapersonnel conflicts. These employee conflicts range from minor annoyances to major interpersonal and departmental struggles. This book represents a proven method for bringing peace to the workplace.

"The civil war occurring in the American workplace is costing organizations hundreds of millions of dollars in lost productivity and lowered worker morale."

Your Peacemaking Role

Any action plan for peace must begin with the players: the Top Guns, the Palace Guards, the Infantry, and the MP Heroes. Each Hero-style can be a powerful force in influencing his or her employees or colleagues to build toward a more

"Peace will not happen by accident. Peace will come to companies that work diligently toward greater psychological understanding of their workforce."

"Leaders, managers, and employees must act their Role Self when interacting with co-workers whose Hero-styles differ from their own."

peaceful work environment. Increased psychological awareness of behavioral style differences by managers and employees alike is key to the American workplace enjoying a more cooperative and productive workforce.

Peace will not happen by accident. Peace will come to companies that work diligently toward greater psychological understanding of their workforce. The more leaders and managers understand the differences between Hero-styles employed in their companies, the more effectively they will lead and manage their workers.

Leaders, managers, and employees must act their Role Self when interacting with co-workers whose Hero-styles differ from their own. We can no longer act unthinkingly or instinctively when facing challenging interpersonal work relationships. When we act "naturally" we stand the chance of misleading, mismanaging, or misbehaving with our people.

We all want to work in organizations where respect, excitement, fairness, and consideration are the rule rather than the exception. When an organization is experiencing disrespectful, unfair, dull, and inconsiderate people, this is a symptom of leaders or managers misleading their Hero-workers. The leaders or managers in these cases have not understood that people's behavior differs consistently and these differences have their origin in early childhood. They will not change easily nor quickly.

Sharon Wegscheider-Cruse, in her 30 years of work with addiction and families, discovered children living in alcoholic, drug-addicted families tended to rely on predictable coping styles to survive. Although these family patterns were first noticed in addictive families, Sharon also found children coping with these same patterns when living in families of "workaholics" or in families where one or both parents were "emotionally absent" (through death, illness, or divorce) from their children. Her models have bearing on the four behavioral styles presented in this book.

In most families, Sharon found children who were the family's firstborns took on the responsibility of making the family proud. To this end, firstborns tend to excel in school and become overachievers in all activities they are involved in. They fear being out of control and strive to always be the person in charge. These children also believe that appearances are everything. When new clothes fads hit the neighborhood, these children will be the first to be seen wearing them. These patterns are similar to this book's behavioral styles—the Top Gun and the Palace Guard.

Sharon also found third-born children often coping as "the Lost Child." These children shunned the spotlight or the notoriety often caused by their older Top Gun or Palace Guard siblings. These children brought relief to the family by not being demanding or making extra work for the parents. The Lost Child is a careful child. They also excel in school, but in ways that are unlike

"The family's first-borns took on the responsibility of making the family proud."

"Third-born children often shunned the spotlight or the notoriety often caused by their older Top Gun or Palace Guard siblings."

their Top Gun or Palace Guard siblings. The Lost Child often becomes the teacher's pet because he or she is so helpful, such a good student, and so little trouble to their teachers. The Lost Child follows directions and is trusted with completing daily responsibilities for their instructors.

My dad, an Infantry Hero, became a business instructor at his high school when there was a shortage of teachers. He was 15 years old! At the age of eight, Dad was driving fuel trucks in downtown St. Paul, Minnesota, fueling office buildings before they opened for business. He was very careful (and he worried a lot), but he was never a problem to his employer. The Lost Child does not want mistakes to occur because of his or her fear of condemnation. No attention is good attention. In some important ways, this early childhood coping pattern fits the Infantry and the MP styles.

Our early childhood experiences shape our adulthood perspectives. Being a Top Gun or Palace Guard suggests these Heroes had the responsibility of being the family's "star." Being an Infantry or MP Hero suggests these individuals became trusted family members who could deliver the goods and bring relief to the family "come rain or shine." As children, we did the best we could, given the limited understanding we all had of our adults' world.

Now that we are adults, we can, unlike our parents, learn to act in our world to our best advantage and for the best of those who work alongside us. We can bring peace to our workplace, by choosing to play the Role that will foster goodwill, encouragement, excitement, and results.

Becoming aware, in order for one to lead, manage, and interact more effectively with their staff, requires leaders, managers, and employees have the knowledge, make the commitment, and take the time to practice desired Role Self behaviors. (See Chapters Eight through Twelve for Real Self versus Role Self information.)

Let us begin again with the Top Gun Hero for you to better understand what steps you can take to increase the sense of peace in your workplace.

THE TOP GUN

Top Guns have particular challenges. Top Gun leaders and employees resist being controlled by others and find most company policies or procedures too restrictive. Motivated by profits, results, and money, Top Guns are internally driven to achieve and see external management pressure as wasted energy. If they agree with the basic directions set by their companies, Top Guns push themselves and others to deliver results. Bonuses and commissions, rather than micro-management or constraining policies, are tremendous incentives for Top Guns. They have faith in their abilities to produce or to win for their companies.

181

Top Gun Strengths

- Entrepreneurial leader or employee
- Big-picture oriented
- Innovative
- Directive organizer
- Decision-maker
- Risk-taker
- Technologically intrigued
- Results-oriented

Top Gun Liabilities

- Resists being controlled or managed
- Overcontrolling
- Demanding and runs over people
- Poor listener
- Intolerant of Palace Guard/Infantry/MP Heroes
- Dislikes completing routine details

"Top Guns' resistance to control does not mean they are un-manageable nor that should they go un-managed."

Top Guns' resistance to control does not mean they are unmanageable nor that should they go unmanaged. Just the opposite. Top Guns *require* strong guidance and well-communicated corporate guidelines for themselves or from others. Otherwise, Top Guns set their own limits and operate independently to gain their results.

Top Guns must decide for themselves when they accept a job, whether or not they can live with their company's constraints. This is a critical de-

182

cision step for Top Guns. Without their commitment to follow a company's purpose and policies,
Top Guns will always find it difficult to fully support their company's direction.

*"Without their commit-
ment to follow a com-
pany's purpose and
policies, Top Guns will
always find it difficult
to fully support their
company's direction."*

Top Gun Career Choices

- Entrepreneur
- Leader
- Manager
- Outside sales
- Concept or financial sales

Top Guns require competitive challenges
where they can put their resolve and strong need
to control to work for themselves or for strong management. If poorly managed, Top Guns become
internal threats inside their organizations. They
defy organizational charts and strive to control
those managers who attempt to manage the Top
Guns.

The following chart is a compatibility chart
indicating a Top Gun's ease of relating to the other
three Hero-styles. Top Guns have to pay particular attention to establishing positive work relationships to maximize corporate peace and bottom-
line profits. Once aware of the Top Guns' land
mines and how to avoid them, these strong entrepreneurial types can be powerful contributors to
peace, work, and world order.

| Styles | | Excellent | | Good | | Fair | | Poor | |
Boss	Employee	1	2	3	4	5	6	7	8
Top Gun	Top Gun	✓		+	O		★ ★		
Top Gun	Palace Guard			+ O	✓	★	★		
Top Gun	Infantry		+ O★		✓		★		
Top Gun	MP		★	O +	✓	★			

CHARACTERISTICS KEY:

O Human Relations ✓ Management Compatibility
★ Work Tasks ★ Results Without Systems
+ Results With Systems

"Top Guns tend to form excellent human relationships with the Infantry."

For example, this compatibility chart is for Top Gun bosses. If you follow the (O) symbol, you will notice Top Guns tend to form excellent human relationships with the Infantry. However, Top Guns rate only "fair" results when leading the Infantry without business systems in place (★). Top Guns expect everyone to be risk-takers, controlling, and aggressive when the Top Guns want them to be. Yet, the Infantry are more reserved and thorough Heroes rather than aggressive or risk-taking. This difference in workstyles is an indicator of where Top Guns can alter their Real Self style to a different Role Self style. As a Role Self manager, Top Guns can provide their Infantry staff with business systems through which the Infantry can get results. This management method, Top Guns playing a Role of systematic leadership, ensures the Infantry can get the Top Guns' results.

If as an employee you are reading this book, you have already identified your boss's Hero-style. There are three more compatibility charts following this Top Gun chart. Locate the compatibility chart on the following pages that corresponds to your employer's Hero-style. If your boss is a Top Gun, the Top Gun compatibility chart applies to you. Just match your boss to your Hero-style (Infantry, Palace Guard, or MP) on the same chart. Follow the five symbols describing work and home compatibility to understand how suited your style at work matches or misses that of your employer's. Is your actual relationship, for example in work tasks, more positive than what is shown on the chart? If so, that is excellent! You have learned how to work under your boss's Hero-style (workstyle). If your work task relationship is negative, then you have an opportunity to alter your Real Self style to a more compatible Role Self style to better serve your boss. You decide the Role you need to play. This decision is "Employee Empowerment" in action!

THE PALACE GUARD

Palace Guards are either loved or hated, just as Top Guns are either respected or feared. Having a halfway experience with these powerful Palace Guard Heroes is difficult. Palace Guards can make work *fun*, if we can put up with the occasional emotional roller coaster ride that Palace Guards are famous for. When Palace Guards are happy, they are very, very happy. However, when they are sad, they are very, very sad.

"Palace Guards are either loved or hated, just as Top Guns are either respected or feared."

Projecting positive self-images, Palace Guards are exceptional marketers of themselves, their companies, or their products and services. They know how to create quick rapport with prospective customers and how to soothe the feathers of demanding repeat customers. Palace Guards know image *sells*. Product knowledge and industry knowledge are important to Palace Guards, but more important is how the Palace Guard appears to the customer. Appearance is everything.

Palace Guard Strengths

- Marketer of self or company
- Persuasive communicator
- Team builder
- Enthusiastic
- Motivating
- Optimistic
- Organizer of others

Excellent presenters, Palace Guards are often tapped to be the company's spokesperson. Easy conversationalists, quick on their feet with ad-lib comments, Palace Guards never seem lost for words. They are exemplary Hero models to their audiences: sound successful, look successful, and appear to exude success when with others.

However, Palace Guards can be quick to condemn other Heroes since the other three Hero-styles—Top Guns, Infantry, and MP's—are not as impressive as Palace Guards. Palace Guards look for a person's visual brightness, their verbal quickness, their strict adherence to trends. When another Hero falls short in these key appearance categories, Palace Guards are relentless in their ridicule.

Palace Guard Liabilities

- Low objectivity
- Manipulative
- Emotionally demanding
- Fears rejection associated with cold calling
- Poor listener

Palace Guards need careers in which they experience high degrees of freedom and acceptance from others. They thrive when they have ready-made audiences or strong marketing support.

Palace Guard Career Choices

- Trainer
- Marketing
- Public relations
- High-profile sales
- Creative sales
- Advertising

Palace Guards need jobs that offer them opportunity, acceptance, variety, and monetary

187

rewards. Careers that provide these positive attributes, as well as interesting people to work with, are much sought after by Palace Guards.

To better understand which Hero-style Palace Guards naturally accept and those Heroes the Palace Guard rejects, the following compatibility chart provides a helpful map.

Styles		Excellent		Good		Fair		Poor	
Boss	Employee	1	2	3	4	5	6	7	8
Palace	Top					O			
Guard	Gun			+		✓★		★	
Palace	Palace		✓	O		★		★	
Guard	Guard			+					
Palace									
Guard	Infantry	★	+	O		★	✓		
Palace									
Guard	MP		+	O	★	★	✓		

CHARACTERISTICS KEY:

O Human Relations   ✓ Management Compatibility

★ Work Tasks   ✩ Results Without Systems

                             + Results With Systems

As their compatibility chart indicates, Palace Guards form few "excellent" human relationships (O). Though Palace Guards thrive on people contact, they tend to form very few close personal friendships with others. This paradox may be better understood when the reader recalls that Palace Guards fear rejection. Due to their sensitivity to rejection, the Palace Guards carefully allow others to get close to them.

THE INFANTRY

Tried and true, the Infantry are the dependable and unsung Heroes of the workplace. Often going unnoticed, the Infantry continue to perform consistently in their jobs with little fanfare. This lack of fanfare may be a relief to the Infantry worker who is otherwise surrounded by Top Guns and Palace Guards.

The Infantry become noticeably vocal, only when there is a fairness issue. Then, the Infantry, too, can become "squeaky wheels." Without a fairness issue surfacing, the Infantry go about their business quietly, sometimes never getting the full attention due to them for their company contributions.

"The Infantry become noticeably vocal, only when there is a fairness issue."

However, being a "forgotten Hero" is the Role Infantry Heroes are most comfortable performing. Infantry *love* low profiles. Lower profiles mean less risk to them personally or professionally. Infantry are not natural risk-takers and only will assume this Role under extreme business circumstances or family pressures. Then, they can become Heroes in the true sense of the word.

Infantry Strengths

- Systems-oriented
- Mentor
- Leads from knowledge
- Patient listener
- Tolerant of other Heroes

189

- Coach and team player
- Service-minded
- Completing complex routines

Paradoxically, it is when the Infantry take well-calculated risks at work that the organization finally recognizes their value. Their expertise and knowledge of their industries or organizations can be strong, but hidden assets.

Infantry Liabilities

- Low tolerance for risks
- Dislikes sudden change
- Peacekeeper
- Wed to systems
- Reserved communicator

"Infantry leaders need business systems or trusted mentors."

Infantry leaders need business systems or trusted mentors to maintain their focus on organizational profits rather than focusing on keeping the peace. Just being knowledgeable about the organization's products and services is not enough for Infantry employers and managers to effectively keep their focus on making a business profit.

However, it is because of their knowledge that the Infantry are tapped as leaders for their organizations. Unwilling leaders, the Infantry, more than the other three Hero-styles, benefit most from practicing established management systems. Learning to lead people for bottom-line, measurable results is key to maximizing Infantry leaders' performances.

190

Infantry Career Choices

- Education
- Science or medicine
- Sports or musicians
- Entertainment
- Computers
- Service industries
- Administration

The Infantry seek careers in which they can practice their well-formed skills in a harmonious work environment. They appreciate working alongside other Heroes, especially when they *all* contribute cooperatively to make results happen.

The following compatibility chart shows the degree to which the Infantry get along with other Heroes and their need for Heroes to lead them.

| Styles | | Excellent | | Good | | Fair | | Poor | |
Boss	Employee	1	2	3	4	5	6	7	8
Infantry	Top				O			✓	
	Gun				+			★★	
Infantry	Palace						✓		
	Guard	O	+	★			★		
Infantry	Infantry		★						
		+	O	✓		★			
Infantry	MP			O					
				+★	✓	★			

CHARACTERISTICS KEY:
O Human Relations   ✓ Management Compatibility
★ Work Tasks   ☆ Results Without Systems
                        + Results With Systems

If the reader is an Infantry Hero, please notice how more effective you can be when you manage others through systems (+). Identify measurable objectives that focus your management involvement with your staff. By staying alert to actual performance, you can avoid becoming embroiled in civil warfare with your more emotional Palace Guards, your demanding Top Guns, or your judgmental MP's.

THE MILITARY POLICE (MP)

The MP thrive on perfection. They love everything at work to be done right, on time, and with no errors. This often means MP's have difficulty working with anyone who does not view work rules, procedures, time deadlines, and achieving accuracy as essential. Unfortunately, many people do not live up to the incredibly high MP expectations. MP employees and managers on their personal scoreboard silently tally disorganized employees or managers, sloppy offices, and administrative mistakes.

MP employees and managers are organizations' quality-control professionals. MP's work to produce results that every Top Gun, Palace Guard, or Infantry would be proud of. MP's spend much energy carrying out the plans of others, diligently assuring everyone of the quality of the output.

MP Strengths

- Quality-oriented
- Procedurally analytical
- Leads from knowledge
- Thorough follow-through
- Accurate and detailed
- Conscientious
- Rules-oriented

MP individuals thrive in structured work-settings where they can carefully plan before meeting their responsibilities. Unwilling to compromise quality for time, MP employees risk taking more time to complete projects rather than rush their deadlines.

MP Liabilities

- Perfectionist
- Judgmental and blaming
- Worrier and poor prioritizer
- Resists change
- Procrastinates

MP individuals require strong leadership to perform or to lead others. In predictable work environments, MP's can better assure themselves that everything can be done, on time and correctly.

When chaos reins, MP's become highly anxious and prefer doing nothing rather than risk errors. When MP managers become disorganized, it is a signal they are overwhelmed by their work demands. Unable to rank tasks for priority, MP's will require help from others in prioritizing their responsibilities. MP's often see *everything* as important.

MP Career Choices

· Technical management
· Administration
· Science and education
· Entertainment and sports
· Law enforcement and military
· Finance and accounting

MP's like law and order. Careers that offer strong dosages of both attract MP's like bees to honey. Companies that run their organization through well established and publicized employee and operations policy manuals also assure MP's of safety and security. When everyone knows the rules and is expected uniformly to abide by them, MP's experience a "level playing field."

MP's have a love/hate relationship with Top Guns and Palace Guards. MP's love the risks that Top Guns take for the MP's, and they love the excitement Palace Guards create around them. However, both Top Guns and Palace Guards are nonchalant toward order and structure. Their

"*When everyone knows the rules and is expected uniformly to abide by them, MP's experience a 'level playing field'.*"

nonchalance creates extreme anxieties for the MP. It is because MP's fear their order and predictability could be sacrificed, that MP's also hate being around loose Top Guns or change-up artists like Palace Guards.

The following compatibility chart indicates with whom the MP's best relate:

Styles		Excellent		Good		Fair		Poor	
Boss	Employee	1	2	3	4	5	6	7	8
MP	Top Gun		O +				✓ ★		
						★	★		
MP	Palace Guard		+	O		★ ★	✓		
MP	Infantry		+ ✓	★	O	★			
MP	MP		+ O	★	✓		★		

CHARACTERISTICS KEY:
O Human Relations   ✓ Management Compatibility
★ Work Tasks   ★ Results Without Systems
    + Results With Systems

MP bosses may notice their management effectiveness (✓) rates "excellent" to "good" with the Infantry and other MP's. However, with Top Gun and Palace Guard employees, MP bosses rate only "fair." MP's tend to be perceived as too judgmental, too picky, or big worry-warts by many Top Guns and Palace Guards. Therefore, for MP bosses to gain their management results, they must utilize performance and management systems for which a *range* of performance goals are set for their employees. For example, set the minimum standards for performance that an employee can achieve and still keep his or her job. Separate out realistic standards of performance from the idealistic or optimistic performance standards. When managing Top Guns and Palace Guards realistically, MP bosses can keep their eye on performance expectations that are achievable and can become encouraging managers rather than demotivating managers to their employees.

SUMMARY

"When you began reading this book, you were walking unaided, through battlefields of the corporate American civil war."

When you began reading this book, you were walking blind, through battlefields of the corporate American civil war. The war being waged in American industries is for international economic supremacy. It is a bloody battle, affecting millions of workers who have already experienced loss of jobs and destruction of careers, while witnessing thousands of big and small companies biting the dust. Hopelessness replaces hope and fear cloaks our lives.

This book is intended to remove its readers' blindfolds when navigating the minefields posed by changing companies, changing workforces, changing jobs, and changing careers. We need to see what we are facing as businesses shift from operating in a national economy to organizations going head-to-head with their foreign competitors. The new emerging business paradigm will enable companies to gain and maintain global competitiveness. These shifts will continue well into the twenty-first century.

Announcement of the paradigm's pending arrival is best illustrated in the form of early labor statistics. The U.S. Bureau of Labor reported that between 1989 and 1992 more than 10.1 million American employees lost jobs. This rate of job loss was 35 percent higher than the previous four years. Since 1992, the rate of job loss has remained high, indicating a continued period of employment transition.

"Lightning-fast changes are replacing everything we learned to rely upon in our work lives."

You are one of hundreds of thousands of employers or employees who struggle daily to make sense of a business world "gone south." Lightning-fast changes are replacing everything we learned to rely upon in our work lives.

Fortune 500 companies continue to disappear from our industrial landscapes. Companies are relocating from large cities to underdeveloped localities to reach cheaper, natural resources and lower wage scales. Jobs continue to dry up, work skills become obsolete overnight, and information buries us. We look for answers in familiar places and find only more unfamiliar questions.

What is happening to American industry? Can we successfully compete with foreign companies who employ cheap labor and produce rapid technological developments that make many of our American products too expensive? Can we afford the American worker? If not, what is to become of us?

"What do we need to learn to compete in the new, global economy?"

What do we need to learn to compete in the new, global economy? As "jobs" go away, what does

197

this mean for millions of us still employed by others? Many organizations are running "leaner and meaner" to survive the global economic competition.

How can we remain hopeful when everything affecting our dreams, our hopes, our jobs, and our financial security is threatened?

This book is a map for finding hidden treasures. By applying the knowledge gained from this book, you can:

- Better understand how to increase your work effectiveness
- Cope with the onslaught of changing workplaces, changing careers, and changing employee groups
- More artfully communicate with peers and other employees
- Participate in teams more productively
- Lead or manage employees with greater confidence

"This book provides you with methods that let you proactively participate in the reduction of the civil war in the American workplace."

This book provides you with methods that let you proactively participate in the reduction of the *civil war in the American workplace.*

FINAL REVIEW

This book was designed to engage the reader in an interactive exploration of themselves and those with whom they work. Specifically the book in-

198

vited you, the reader, to interact with the information to better understand the behavioral dynamics of yourself, your fellow employees, and your workplace.

By selecting adjectives in Chapter Two that best described your natural behavioral style, you were guided to select the Hero-style that best described your approach to work today. Some readers may have selected the Top Gun Hero as most like themselves, other readers may have selected the Palace Guard as exemplary of themselves, still other readers may have selected the Infantry or the MP Hero-style as most descriptive of themselves, behaviorally.

By following your Hero-style as it was described throughout the book, you were introduced in Chapters Four through Seven to not only your own work strengths and liabilities, but also to the work strengths and liabilities of the other three Heroes.

After reading through the book's sections that applied to your Hero-style, you were invited to *reread* the Hero-style sections to recognize the Hero-styles of other people with whom you work. By understanding the behavioral needs of those individuals you work with or work for, you are better equipped to proactively avoid engaging in work conflicts.

"By understanding the behavioral needs of those individuals you work with or work for, you are better equipped to proactively avoid engaging in work conflicts."

I introduced the behavioral concept of Real Self versus Role Self in Chapters Nine through Twelve. In spending years consulting with hundreds of organizations throughout the North

American continent, I found people who loved their jobs because they naturally liked doing the work demanded by the job.

Matching a person's natural Hero-style, their Real Self to the behavior demanded by the job, soon became a TSI hiring concept. Practicing this Real Self job matching concept has proven immensely successful for thousands of our hiring managers. They report their increased hiring successes, turnover reduction, and increased performance and production as a result of matching people's Real Self behavior—their Hero-style—to the behavior demanded by the job.

Role Self Concept

However, in my consulting travels I have also found thousands of employers and employees unhappy at work due to a mismatch of the person's Hero-style to the behavior demanded by the job. This book recounts these stories in sometimes humorous details. However, the mismatch experience, as lived by our clients, has been more distressing than funny. What were their managers' options when faced with a mismatch of job to Real Self behavior? Fire the poor slobs? Heck, no!

This is where our concept of Role Self is so powerful. When faced with a mismatch of Hero-

200

styles to their job demands, managers and employees alike are given training in Role Self performance.

By better understanding work strengths and work liabilities of mismatched employees' Real Self behavior and the behavior demanded by the job, managers are better equipped to apply the Role Self concept. Which Role Self style needs to be played by the manager or the employee will be identified by the type of job they hold in the organization. The type of job an individual holds places different pressures on the person to act according to their job's expected result.

"Which Role Self style needs to be played by the manager or the employee will be identified by the type of job they hold."

For example, if a job demands employees to pay attention to detail and individuals holding the job *hate detail work*, the Role Self option for the employees is to *act as if* they can do detail work. The reality is employees have no choice—do the job or lose the job. The difference made to employees by their electing to use their Role Self is that they will experience being more in charge of their own behavior and they can complete their detail assignments.

Also, managers' Role Self selection will depend upon what Hero-styles their employees exhibit as their Real Self Hero-style.

For example, if you tend to be impatient, like a typical Top Gun, but your employee (or manager) is an Infantry Hero, your Role Self option will be that of a patient listener. Or you will introduce change to your Infantry employee or manager in incremental steps rather than surprise them with sudden or unplanned change.

Once you have identified your need to act as a Role Self with one individual and put into practice what you have read in this book, you will find you have greater flexibility to respond to others, *as they need you to be.* By practicing behavior appreciated by those who work alongside or for you, you will find increased mutual understanding and mutual respect. You have found a way to end your company's civil war.

Stopping the Civil War

"Reducing any civil war occurring in your company requires you to take the first step."

Reducing any civil war occurring in your company requires you to take the first step. Stopping the war rests with you. Why? Because you have read this book and have the knowledge that other people in your company do not have.

If you want help in bringing greater peace throughout your workplace, ask your employees or colleagues to read this book. Then, they too will have knowledge from which to bring greater peace and with peace, greater prosperity for all.

Finally, we can offer help in turning your "civil war" into a lasting peace. We offer seminars, processes, and systems to help you gain understanding of your people, how to select them, how to "motivate" them, and how to focus everyone on the organization's needs for the future.

AFTERWORD

In this book, I have sought to illustrate the power of the human personality in shaping and resolving civil wars in the workplace. Throughout the book I have given numerous examples of actual conflicts between business people and how these conflicts had their origins in personality differences. When experiencing stressful situations, many of us behave at our worst rather than at our best. In the turbulent changes occurring in industry throughout North America, employers and employees are experiencing loss of loyalty, security, and hope. Leaders are hard-pressed keeping their organizations financially viable and globally competitive. Laying-off millions of American workers may have been (and continues to be) the leaders' heaviest burden.

In these difficult times, all of us need to be proactive in gaining the employment and profitability edge in the next century. The future bodes well only if we are willing today to minimize our work behavior liabilities and maximize those interpersonal skills that will add to our continued marketability as employees or leaders of industry.

If you have found this book's message helpful, then I ask you to take the following steps:

· Make a list of those people at work with whom you are currently experiencing conflict. Then, list beliefs you hold about your job that you think essential to performing well in your organization. For example, you may believe you must do every job "perfectly" in order for you to experience job satisfaction. Or, you may believe you must be liked by everyone in order to be successful in your job.

· Then following each belief, list your behaviors that *others* would observe about you that would indicate your "perfectionistic" or "need to be liked" beliefs in action. For example, do you double check or triple check your work, becoming a bottleneck to the workflow? Do you find yourself talking more rather than listening to others?

· Next, compare those employees, co-workers, or peers that have had difficulty working for or alongside you to your belief/behaviors list. As you read over your lists, you may notice how your beliefs and your behaviors help you keep the peace at work or cause you to experience work conflicts. Which of your behaviors (and/or beliefs) would you be willing to alter to resolve your co-worker or employee conflict?

This exercise allows you to assess your work beliefs and their relationship to your self-defeating workplace behaviors. Taking responsibility for your behavior and your job performance is a valuable twenty-first century work skill. Unexamined beliefs and unrestrained behavior are too dangerous in these times of global industrial transformation. Peace and prosperity in the workplace can only visit those individuals who possess work skills which include self-awareness, taking responsibility, flexibility, and sensitivity toward others.

REFERENCES

William Bridges, "The End of the Job," *Fortune*, September 19, 1994, pp. 62-74.

Burrough, Bryan & John Helyar, *Barbarians at the Gate: The Fall of RJR Nabisco*, Harper & Row, 1990.

Henry Gleitman, *Psychology*, Norton, 1981.

Howard G. Haas with Bob Tamarkin, *The Leader Within*, Harper Collins Publishers, Inc., 1992.

Harry Levinson, "Why the Behemoths Fell," *American Psychologist*, Volume 49, Number 5, May 1994, pp. 428-439.

Alexander Pope, "An Essay from Man," *The Columbia Granger's Dictionary of Poetry Quotations*, Columbia University Press, 1992.

Virginia Satir, *Peoplemaking*, Science and Behavior Books, Inc., 1972.

Steve Stecklow, "Management 101," *The Wall Street Journal*, December 9, 1994, pp. A1 and A10.

Sharon Wegscheider, *The Family Trap*, 1976.